SELF-WORTH

Inspirational Psychology for Self-Ecology!

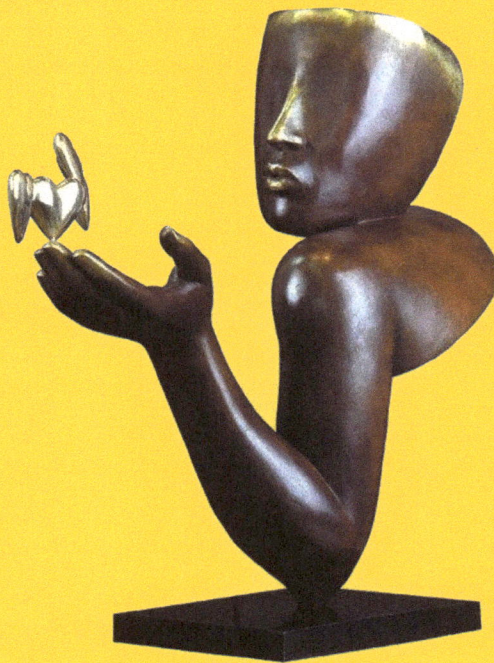

Authenticate Your Unique Fate!

Dr. Rimaletta Ray

ISBN 978-1-952302-24-4 (sc)
ISBN 978-1-952302-25-1 (e)

Library of Congress Control Number: 2020918581

Attitude of Gratitude

All the pictures of the sculptures in this book are by a great French sculptor Etienne Pirot.

My heartfelt gratitude to the master for their incredible beauty and the conceptual value, helping to illustrate the concepts of my book.

Self-Worth is the Accumulation of the Inner Integrity Force!

"It's much more difficult to be kind and decisive than just intelligent, but inactive!" (Jeff Bezos)

"Engineering yourself is the process of becoming conscious of being human."(Sadhguru)

Only the Beauty of Life that's Consciously Perceived will Save the World!"(Nickolas Roerich)

<u>Book Incentive</u>

Life is Going on, and It's Great in Your Own Form!

Be the Station for Your Own Inspiration!

Self-Respect is Me; Self-Respect is My Philosophy!

"It's time to awaken your evolutionary potential and activate your superhuman capabilities."

(Gregg Braden)

Benefit from My Inspirational Outfit! Be Life-Upbeat!

1. To Live Right is to Accumulate the Self-Worth Might!

I'm Unique in Every

Stance.

I was born but only

Once!

There wasn't, there

isn't,

There won't ever be

Anyone like Me!

Discover your exceptionality without vanity!

"The calling for your life is irrevocable."

(" The Words of Christ', 1977)

I Know Who I am Self-Worth Wise, but it's More Vital for Me to figure out

What I am Not!

2. Make Your Heart Smart and the Mind Kind. Be One of a Kind!

Solarize Your Soul
with Intelligence, Kindness, and Self-Control!

Self-Worth is Not Vanity;
It's the Essence of Your Personality
with a Tangible Sense of Individuality!

This book is just <u>an inspirational booster,</u> reminding you of the most vital path in life – the path of **Self-Resurrection** *that is a structural entity as everything else in life. Only the one who exceeds his / her potential, who says:* **"I Can, I Must, and I Will!"** *has the sense of* **Self-Worth** *on this Earth. You need to create your own road map on the way, discarding the invisible excess baggage that slows down the journey to yourself <u>on the newly created path of digitally paved life.</u>*

Become a Much Wiser Self-Actualizer!

3. Being the Best is a Tough Test!

Being the best

Is a tough test!

But don't you fret it,

Go for it and get it!

Whatever it might be,

Add to it some personal glee!

Fear is but the food

That poisons your intentions and a good mood!

It freezes your mind and body

And releases a self-pity zombie!

To conquer the fear foe,

Give it a striking blow!

Cut it in the bud,

And be done with that!

Shakespeare was not wrong,

"A light heart lives long!"

So, harmonize your inner guts

And enjoy life in all its parts!

"It's not enough to be the best. Be the Only!"

(Steve Jobs)

Our Life-Education should be based on New Knowledge and Inspiration!

4. Inspirational Psychology for Self-Ecology

The book " *Self-Worth* " is a logical continuation of the set of my five books on the system of holistic **Self-Resurrection**, presented in five philosophical levels – *physical, emotional, mental, spiritual, and universal* consequentially. Protect your inner world with the holistic fort and the ***Inspirational Psychology for Self-Ecology.*** *(www.language-fitness.com / the video on five books is in Self-Resurrection Section)*

The Route and the Stages of Self-Resurrection:

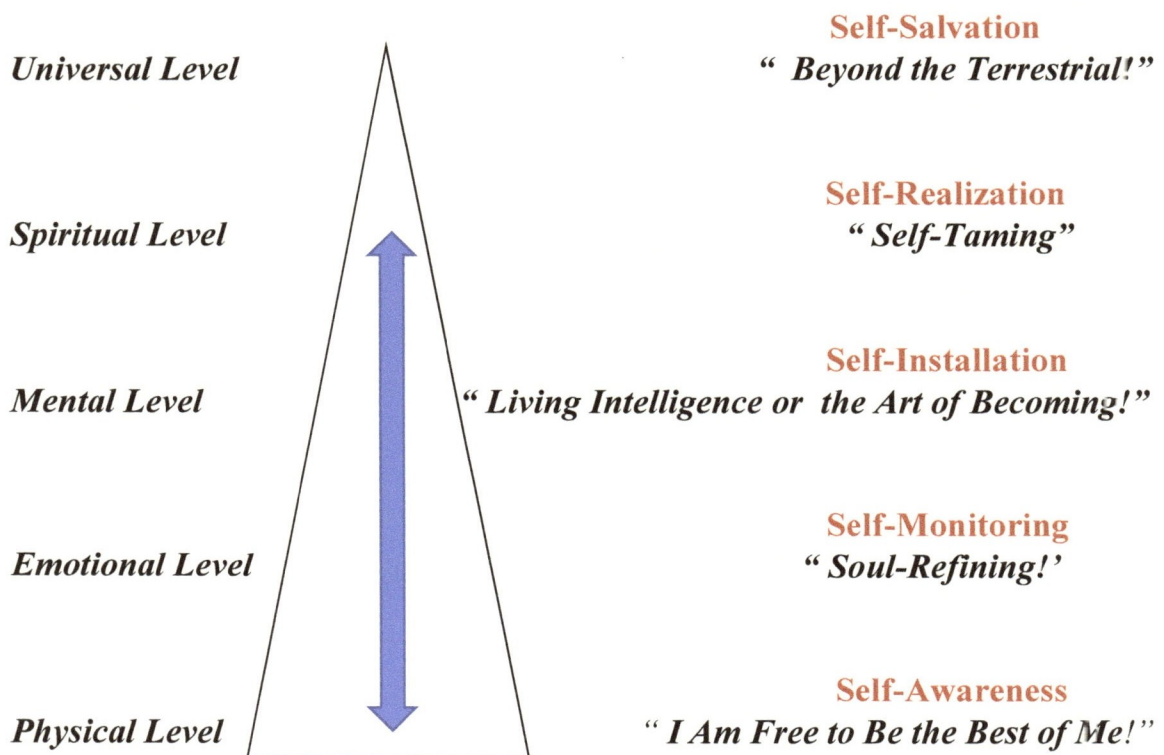

Universal Level	**Self-Salvation** *" Beyond the Terrestrial!"*
Spiritual Level	**Self-Realization** *" Self-Taming"*
Mental Level	**Self-Installation** *" Living Intelligence or the Art of Becoming!"*
Emotional Level	**Self-Monitoring** *" Soul-Refining!'*
Physical Level	**Self-Awareness** *" I Am Free to Be the Best of Me!"*

For knowledge to be useful, it must be holistically applied!

The books lead you through *a holistic exposition of the physical, emotional, mental, spiritual, and universal fundamentals of life,* directing you to a ***deeper fulfillment of your exceptionality*** that gradually shapes itself into a fuller realization of your life's goal.

Continue Your Self-Installation Mindfully and with Elation!

Table of Contents

(Me and the Bits of My Philosophy!)

11. *Launch Yourself to the Universal Life Energy Spell!*
12. *Self-Growth Agenda Must be Unique, Not Bleak!*
13. *I'm My Best Friend ; I'm My Beginning and My End!*
14. *Your Name is the Passport of Your Self-Worth*
15. *To Become the Most Fulfilled and Loving Self, Love Yourself!*
16. *The Cyber Security is Your Space and Time Unity*
17. *Keep Your Soul in the Holistically Monitored Self-Control!*
18. *Selection + Organization = Self-Construction in Action!*
19. *Indifference and Impersonality are the Products of Self-Vanity!*
20. *Be Your Own Best Friend!*
21. *Manage Yourself by Re-Programming Your Cells!*

Stage Two - Self-Worth Monitoring *(Emotional level of Self-Scanning)* ----pp.68-95

1. *Being Starstruck is a Special Personality Mark!*
2. *We are Unique in Ever Stance; We Can Live but Only Once!*
3. *The Quality of life is a Newly Discovered Self-Might!*
4. *In My Life Quest, I'm the Best!*
5. *Stabilize Your Emotional Surf; Calm Yourself!*
6. *To Build up an Emotional Fort, Master Your Love World!*
7. *Self-Worth is Our Love's Boss!*
8. *Holistic Self-Worth Accumulation is based on Love Elation!*
9. *Love-Gaining is in Self-Taming!*
10. *Love Domain is in Every Vein!*
11. *Don't Be Love Negligent; Be love Intelligent!*
12. *Marriage is the Test for Self-Worth Wealth!*
13. *Love Consciousness is a Mess!*
14. *Your Personal Psychology is in Love Ecology.*
15. *Marriage Gravity is not Built on Self-Vanity!*
16. *Love Infinity Develops Character Ability*
17. *Love Gravity is formed by the Fractals of Self-Symmetry*
18. *Expand the Inner Circle of Resistance to the Poison of Life!*
19. *To Be a Self-Programmed Love Cell, Tame Yourself!*
20. *Forgiveness doesn't Change the Past, but It does Change the Future!*
21. *To Change the Karma Role, Take Care of Your Soul!*
22. *Emotional Gravity is Charged by Wisdom, not by Love Treason!*

Stage Three – Self-Worth Installation *(Mental level of Self-Scanning* ----pp.96-110

1. *"Mind Over Matter" is Our Self-Worth Strata!*
2. *Vistas of Intelligence to Mount*
3. *Intelligence and Self-Worth Must be in Force!*
4. *Self-Installation is the Process of Self-Worth Formation!*
5. *Knowledge Provides Mental Fruition and Intuition!*
6. *A Man is the Product of His Thoughts and Words.*
7. *Don't Get Insane; Befriend Your Brain!*
8. *Be God-Centered and Intelligence Absorbing!*
9. *Don't Think and Speak in Haste; It's Your Mind's Waste!*
10. *My Global Role is to Holistically Reform My Soul!*

11. *Launch Yourself to the life's Energy Spell!*
12. *Mobilize a Lot of Zest for Being the Best!*

1. *Religiousness and Self-Worth are in Opposition since Birth!*
2. *Self-Worth is Connected to Christ's Media Force.*
3. *Negative Sensationalism is Killing Self-Growth.*
4. *We need to Become Spiritualized and Godly Wise!*
5. *Conscience Manifests in the Best!*
6. *Bless People in Your Mind. Be One of a Kind!*
7. *De-Magnetization of Self- Worth*
8. *Habits Stability Needs to be tuned into Skills Nobility!*
9. *Your Personal Goal's Right is Your Spiritual Might!*
10. *Outshine Those that are Vile; Shine!*
11. *Praying is Self-Worth Gaining!*
12. *Idealism is Our Best Self-Forming "izm"*

1. *The Soul's Salvation is in the Universal Realization!*
2. *Universal Awakening is the Path of the Elite Minds*
3. *Integrity is the Wholeness of Oneness!*
4. *Be Bold! Change Your Society Programmed Mold!*
5. *To Get the Universal Inkling, Change the Culture of Thinking!*
6. *Don't Let Anyone Erode Your Spiritual Mold!*
7. *Launch the Program of Elation and Rejuvenation!*
8. *Scientific Literacy is needed Now - WOW!*
9. *Self-Scanning is Self-Worth Refining!*
10. *The Matrix of Self- Worth Formation*
11. *Accept Your Life in its Entire Mass!*

Internalize Your Emotions and Externalize the Mind!

1. *To Live or to Survive - that's the Question of the Present-day Life!*
2. *Your Self-Viability Must be in Holistic Unity!*
3. *Generalize – Select - Internalize - Strategize - Actualize! Be Wise1*
4. *Everyone Has a Magic Wand - God's Words at Hand!*
5. *Your Luminosity is in Self- Worth Velocity!*
6. *Don't Ever Turn off the Light in Your Soul! Stay Whole!*
7. *The Route of Self-Resurrection Must be Completed Section by Section!*
8. *My Final Self-Induction*

*Use New Technology to change
your Self-Worth Ecology!*

Education is Not Just Learning,

It's Also Self-Forming!

Book Rationale

Make Self-Ecology Your Personal Psychology!

Your Personal Gravitational Force is in the Self-Worth!

Self-Worth = Dignity + Intelligence + Kindness!

Being Star-struck is a Special Personality Mark!

You Can Roam any Terrain with Self-Worth in Your Vein!

To Build Your Personal Might, Love Your Life!

The Growth of Self-Worth is in the Virtual World of the Planet Earth!

1. Auto-Induction for a Better Life Production

I'm Unique in Ever Stance.

I was Born but only Once!

There wasn't,

There isn't,

There won't ever be

Anyone like Me!

A person of self-worth manages to get rid of his egotistic compulsive nature thanks to self-consciousness that he /she is developing consistently throughout life.

Self-Induction:

My Personal Goal is the Renaissance of the Soul!

2. Life is Me; Life is My Philosophy!

(An Inspirational Booster)

I invited Life for a cup of tea,

And Life started to question me.

-"Why am I here , please, say,

Are you OK?"

-" I think that my life is not right,

And luck is never at my side.

I live as your imposter,

I'm constantly on the Rolla Costa!"

-"I see", retorted Life with a shining glee,

But it's not about Me!

It's the course of the beat of your heart

And the vibrations of the Universe, at that.

All you need is to love Me

And accept the rhythm of the Life's Sea!

You are here at your parent's invitation

And their joint love elation.

So, love yourself

With Me in your every cell

And quickly change your mood –

"You are Not Here for Good!"

3. Gaining the Self-Worth Expertise is Not a Breeze!

To gain self-worth expertise doesn't mean to do the soul's striptease. Your nature knows best what you need to do to help your self-growth seed grow in the *physical, emotional, mental, spiritual, and universal planes* holistically. We need to let **Jesus Christ, Shiva, Allah, or any religious leaders resurrect in us** through technologically enhanced **LIFE LITERACY** obtained in the multi-dimensional self-growth.

The Growth of Self-Worth is a Multi-Dimensional course!

The Holistic Levels of Self-Resurrection: / Stages: /   Books, featuring these stages:

Level		Stage	Book
5. *Universal*	- **Super-*Consciousness.***	**Self-Salvation**	*"Beyond the Terrestrial!"*
4 *Spiritual*	- **Self-Consciousness**	**Self-Realization**	*"Self-Taming!"*
3. *Mental*	- **Mind**	**Self-Installation**	*" Living Intelligence or…"*
2 *Emotional*	- **Spirit**	**Self-Monitoring**	*" Soul-Refining"!*
1. *Physical*	- **Body**	**Self-Awareness**	*"I Am Free to Be the Best…*

Self-Resurrection on the path of fractal self-formation:
(Body+ Spirit+ Mind) + (Self-Consciousness + Universal Consciousness)

My five books or *the Paradigm of Self–Resurrection,* presented above, comprise the **MANUAL OF LIFE** as my modest contribution to the on-growing process of our *spiritually intellectualized maturation* at the time of the exponentially growing technological boom. Each book has its own auto-suggestive motto *(see below)* and together, they comprise the *Geology of Self-Ecology* or the self-coaching program.

You need to remember that *personal magnetism* that we call *charisma* is not the quality we are born with. It's a life-long process of **SELF-TAMING** and *monitored self-growth*, based on self-love and self-respect. A famous digital biologist's, *Dr. Bruce Lipton,* calls on us now, *" Don't wait for the life circumstances to change and make you happy. Be happy to change the life circumstances."*

Build up Your Inner Fort with an Inspirational Word!

4. Self-Growth Force is Magnetized by Growing Self-Worth!

As I have mentioned above, the book *"Self-Worth"* is topping five books on **Self-Resurrection** that make up the holistic paradigm of self-growth consequentially in the *physical, emotional, mental, spiritual, and universal* levels.

"When you have wholeness, you are holy." (*Deepak Chopra*)

The book is meant to back up your sense of self-worth in these dimensions of life. *The rhyming mind-sets* that start and conclude all page-long chunks of information can be uploaded to your smart phone in the file *My Self-Resurrection.* You might want to have some of them at hand to boost your spirit when it sags.

The book features five levels of self-growth as your **SELF-HELP THERAPY,** providing consequentially the blueprint for self-reformation according to your needs and the choice that they dictate in any (*physical, emotional, mental, spiritual, and universal)* levels. My daughter, *Yolanta Lensky,* who has illustrated many of my books, has come up with the term that she thinks characterizes best this structure.

Our personal might is in the" simplexity" of life!

You can read the book consequentially or randomly, cleaning up your self-worth of bad habits and filling it up with new constructive skills. Focus on those sides of your character that need perfection. Be objective when doing that. Self-honesty is essential here.

Self-Worth formation is changing you into what you are NOT!

1) The first book, *"I'm Free to Be the Best of Me!"* ascertains the main guidelines on the path of gaining solid **SELF-AWARENESS** at the initial, physical level of self-creation. *(See Book Incentive above)*

Self- Induction: **In my Life-Quest, I Am the Best!**

2) The second book " *Soul-Refining!"* helps you become more skillful in your emotional maintenance. It inspires you to perform **SELF-**

MONITORING consciously and consistently, and it will instill in you the vital *mind+ heart unity* so it could work in sync with the Universal Intelligence that we all call God.

Self- Induction: *Make your heart smart t and the mind kind!*

3) The mental level is the central one and it is being featured by the third *Book Excellence Award* winner - *"Living Intelligence or the Art of Becoming!"* Putting the mental framework in shape and enriching it in ten most essential intelligences holistically will back you up in your professional **SELF-INSTALLATION** in life.

Self -Induction: *The Greatest Art of all is to Self-Install!*

4) Next, you are invited to round off the process of never-ending spiritual maturation ,working with the book *"Self-Taming!"* The book will help you go beyond the religious limitations and use your growing self-consciousness as the path to full **SELF-REALIZATION**.

Self -Induction: *Life-Gaining is in Self-Taming!*

5) Finally, you can use the acquired wisdom in the fifth book" *Beyond the Terrestrial,"* featuring the universal plane of life. Focusing integrally on each level of **SELF-SALVATION** in the technologically backed-up environment will ascertain your exceptionality that forms your dream of Self Realization in life.

Self-Induction: *"As it is Above, so it is below!"*

To conclude, self-worth comprises a person's **INNER GRAVITY** without which there is no self-growth. I invite you to pursue this goal centralized by intelligence, grace ,and nobility of the spirit. enhanced with new knowledge and a deeper sense of self-worth, taking you beyond the boundaries of the common into the unpredictability of the future. We are on the path of becoming *"beyond the terrestrial"* people.

"Go beyond, fully beyond, completely beyond!" (Buddhist Mantra)

Consciously Infuse Your Self-Realization Fuse!

5. Life Literacy Must Be Devoid of Stagnation and Obstinacy!

The beautiful words below by *William Shakespeare* from "*Hamlet*" are the timeless call on us *to exceed personal limitations* that we impose on ourselves and never stop changing and growing.

"A man's reach should exceed his grasp!"

I have written sixteen books on the *Inspirational Psychology of Self-Ecology*, but the most meaningful of them are five books, featuring *Self-Resurrection* as the holistic structure of self-growth. I've crowned those five books with the book *"Love Ecology"* in which I'm trying to add my bit to putting an end to the process of love degradation and restore the authenticity of love in the society.

However, I realize that no theory of whatever inspirational, educational and philosophical nature it might be can change a person unless he / she has accumulated the sense of **SELF-WORTH** or *personal magnetism* and ascertained the personal value of his / her life.

The question "*What's he / she worth?* that is normally answered in the USA as – "*He's 4 million /etc. worth*" will take its true value only based on the quality of a person's life that is at present swamped in a wedding haze, crazy fun, deceptive relationships, shamelessness, profanity, and a blind chase for money.

The authenticity of our thoughts, feelings , and actions is buried now in pretentiousness, fake niceness, and the habit to present oneself for someone else or to win the attention of those for whom the "*Shagreen Skin* "of a second personality has totally covered the real one.

In *Honoree De Balzac's* novel, the magic *shagreen skin* promises to fulfill any wish of its owner, shrinking slightly upon the fulfillment of each desire. *But actions must meet consequences!* A person's self-worth gets ruined by *the immediate gratification chase* and the betrayal of his / her dream of full self-fulfillment in the turmoil of life. *So, what is needed for a ruinous self-rotting not to happen?*

This is What this Book is All About.

The Structure of the Book in its Conceptual Nook

An Inspirational Injection For a Better Life Projection

Your Self-Growth must be in the Self-Programming Dose!

Upload your smart phone with a new inspirational tone!

We Have Mis-Wired the Circuitry of our Lives with Life-Negligence and Fun-Spice!

Make the Energy of Light Your Philosophy Inside!

Life is Fragile and Meager. Don't Waste it for a Fun Rigor!

1. The Conceptual Structure of the Book

The conceptional structure of the book is very simple. Each chunk of information is a page long, topped by and concluded with the rhyming mind-sets, presenting it and summing it up. I try to conceptually frame each meaningful paragraph, too, with a highlighted quote or the mind-set that illustrates the concept of the paragraph. The text of the whole book follows the systemic paradigm of all my books:

Synthesis - Analysis - Synthesis!

All the rhyming mind-sets in the book *(the rhyming word goes better inward)* are meant to be easily memorable and technologically friendly. You can upload any of them into your smart phone and use them as **the psychological back-up** for your *physical, emotional, mental, spiritual, or universal* make up. I call the corresponding parts of the book **Stages** and take you through them consequentially.

Thus, I hope to promote the necessity for us to have more life literacy with the **MANUAL OF LIFE** *in five philosophical dimensions* because, as an educator. I see how badly equipped for life our young people are and how inspirational word uplifts my students and friends, my readers and the loved ones. We all need much support of self-worth on the planet Earth!

We need the self-worth guide to accumulate Self-Might!

A rhyming word with the psychological filling resonates with the hearts and minds of my students and helps them take life in stride. I help them realize that life is **matter + intelligence** or consciousness in motion that we've only started tapping into digitally.

Our Spiritual grace is based on the self-worth space!

Self-growth needs to be **conscious, disciplined, and holistically oriented.** We should assess it continuously in the *physical, emotional, mental, spiritual, and universal* dimensions of life on a regular basis. holistically. *(See the video on Self-Resurrection in www. language-fitness.com)*

With the Plan of Action in the Brain, You Can Life-Gain!

2. Self-Worth is a Multi-Dimensional Course!

> **"Most of us never really learn how to wire our lives."**
>
> *(Ravi P.S. Berg)*

It is Life + Living = Self-Coaching!

Life's Worth + Self -Worth = Form + Content of life!

(See the first book on Self-Resurrection- " I'm Free to Be the Best of Me!")

The Fractal of Beings with Spiritualized Intelligence:

Form **+** **Content**

(Body+ Spirit+ Mind) + (Self-Consciousness + Universal Consciousness)

Physical , emotional, mental, spiritual, and universal realms of life

= *Living Intelligence* **+** *Enlightened Self-Consciousness*

= A whole, spiritually intellectualized Self!

(For more on the Spiritual Fractals , see the book "I'm Free to Be the Best of Me!" (physical dimension) www.language-fitness.com

So, our main goal in life is the growth of

the Spiritually Intellectualized Might!

To Live or to Survive? - That's the Question of the Present-Day Life!

3. Vistas of Self-Worth Growth

Self-Worth is the Result of the Holistic Self-Growth!

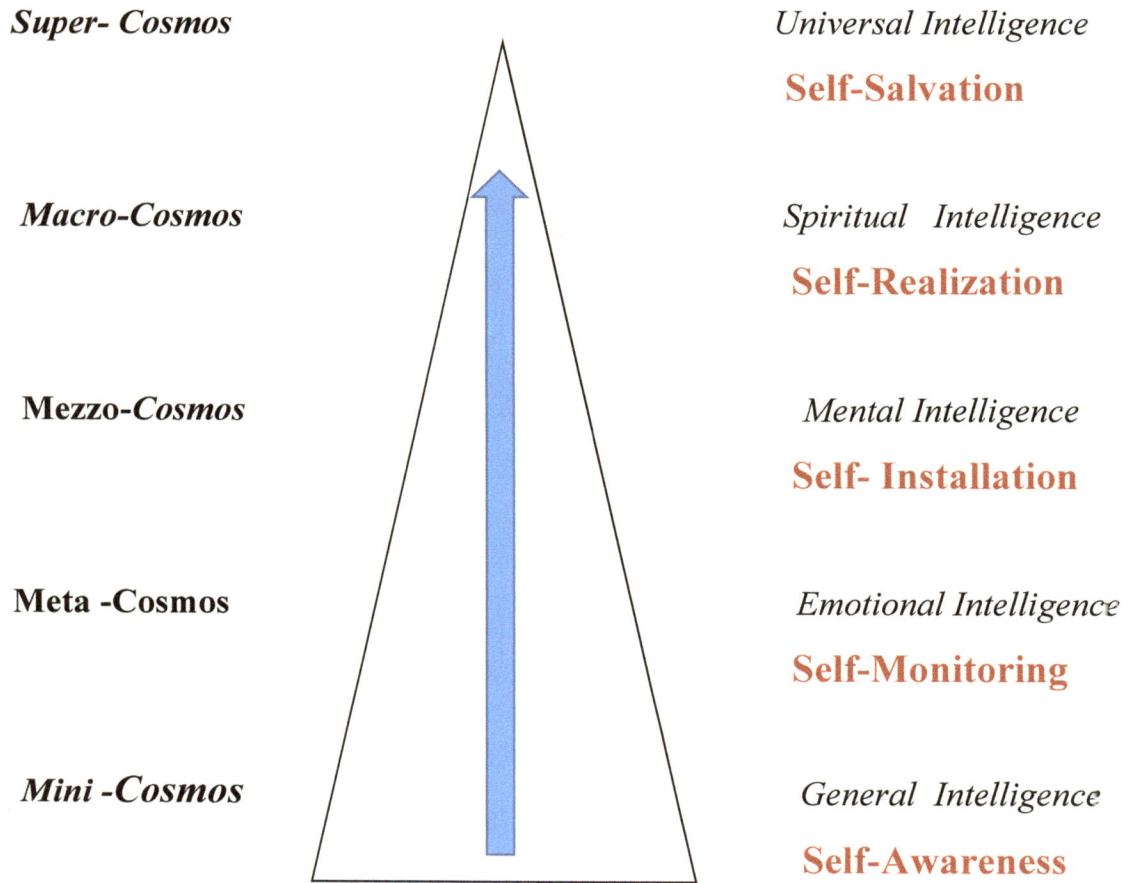

Super- Cosmos		*Universal Intelligence*
		Self-Salvation
Macro-Cosmos		*Spiritual Intelligence*
		Self-Realization
Mezzo-Cosmos		*Mental Intelligence*
		Self- Installation
Meta -Cosmos		*Emotional Intelligence*
		Self-Monitoring
Mini -Cosmos		*General Intelligence*
		Self-Awareness

Integrity is Wholeness in Action! = **Self-Awareness + Self-Monitoring + Self-Installation + Self-Realization + Self-Salvation!**

Only raising self-consciousness can you obtain true *spiritual maturity, personal integrity, and charismatic magnetism* , or the <u>**SELF-WORTH GRAVITY**</u>. These are the prerequisites of <u>*high self-consciousness*</u> that must be the outcome of any one's life. Only having developed high self-consciousness, can you expand your <u>personal informational field</u> and get connected to *" the Universal Informational Field "* (*Dr. John. Hagelin*) or "The Source" *(Dr. Wayne Dyer).*

To Begin Building up a Conscious Self ; Be Yourself!

4. The Conceptual Structure of Life is Beyond Survive!

A self-creation process is both <u>thinking and visualizing</u> the ways of getting more aware of *the conceptual structure of life* in which each and every soul counts as a part of the whole – *the Universal Consciousness of God -* the light at the end of the tunnel that we are heading to. One thing should be stable and inarguable in our search of that light. We need to create ourselves and uplift our consciousness every minute *as spiritualized intelligent beings.*

Information ➡ *Transformation!*

Indeed, it's a never-ending genetic formula, modifying our minds and hearts exponentially. But <u>only the unity of both makes up our souls, our eternal minds</u>. Every soul has a *mental-emotional energy core* that is charged with the intelligence of its owner and that constitutes his / her growing *self-consciousness gravity*. Therefore, your self-consciousness needs to be refined through the process of enriching intelligence, on the one hand, and committing to <u>more rational, heart-based, and noble actions in life</u>, on the other.

It should be kept in mind that developing our intelligence in an inseparable link with the heart, we are constructing the <u>**NEW CONCEPTUAL CONTENT OF LIFE**</u>, new consciousness of the society and the world, destroying the old one and using the entropic energy that is released on this path <u>to decipher new meanings of the</u> **UNIVERSAL TEXT** that we are perceiving digitally now. The digital information that we are learning to digest is enveloping us as *the Universal Intelligence.* We are descripting it from one level of consciousness to the next <u>in an inoperable unity with the heart,</u> developing *"emotional intelligence" (Daniel Goldman)* in sync with general intelligence, enriched with the new technological means.

The Higher a Person's Self-Consciousness, the Nobler his Soul is!

5. Self-Worth Role Models

The avalanche of information on the Internet today provides numerous stories of successful people, urging us to follow their business rules. Unfortunately, these inspiring examples are hardly possible to be applied because the people, like **Nikola Tesla, Steve Jobs, Elon Mask, Jeff Bezos, Jack Ma** and many outstanding scientists, writers, and artists are self-created people that mesmerize us with their bold ideas, amazing entrepreneurial skills, and unbeatable willpower that they developed against all odds. They are "*Beyond the Terrestrial*" people!

They are all extraordinary in one common trait of character. They are all **SELF-WORTH**-oriented people. First and foremost, *they do not fake* their intentions or their excitement with success or disappointment with failures. They are **AUTHENTIC** in their self-value and, most importantly, *the left and right brain hemispheres of these people work in sync*! (*See the book "Beyond the Terrestrial!"*)

Their magnetic power is the unity of the **HEART + MIND** link ,too. These exceptional people do not just follow their heart, or their intuition , as is often noted. I'm sure they follow *the lead of the mind with the heart in sync*. Their intuition connects them to the Universal Intelligence because intuition is the direct line with God.

They might not declare being religious, but they are, for sure, very spiritual people that have the support of the Universal Intelligence, or God in our new, digitally enhanced understanding of the supervision of *the gifted people from the Above and Beyond.*

The self-worth people go beyond, completely beyond, fully beyond!

Also, the main constructive core that these people's personal magnetism is built on is in five holistic dimensions - *Self-Awareness* (physical); *Self-Monitoring* (emotional); *Self-Installation* (mental); *Self-Realization* (spiritual), and *Self-Salvation* (universal). The mind-set they follow is steadfast and starstruck:

I Can...! I Want to...! and I Will...!

6. So, Be Your Best Life's Mate – Invigorate Your Fate!

Self-Induction:

I Do Not Need
To Justify Myself;
I Know Who I Am
In My Every Cell!

Self-Worth means becoming more and more <u>characterful!</u>

The life span of the characterless is getting less, <u>less, and less!</u>

So, overcome the inertia of empty, stereotyped, and <u>mindless living!</u>

Self-Induction:

The Core of My Independent Cell are the Words – "<u>I Love Myself!</u>"

Introduction to Self-Worth Induction

Me and the Bits
of
My Philosophy

Our Personal Might is in the "Simplexity" of Life!

This book is not simply a list of recommended ways to gain self-worth in five dimensions to become unbeatable in life. It presents and establishes the integral science of self-growth as the knowledge which not only leads the individual to a happier life, but also to spiritual advancement and self-evolution.

Inspirational Auto-Induction is the Onto-Genesis of Self-Production!

Life is an Enigma! It Needs to Be Studied, Self-Tamed, and Self-Guarded!

Build up Your Inner Fort with an Inspirational Word!

1. Auto-Suggestive Psychology of Self-Ecology

The Earth is curving space and time, and so are we!

(See the book "Beyond the Terrestrial!" – Universal level of Self-Resurrection)

Life-Elation

is in Ascending the Skies of

Self-Creation!

Self-Worth is the

Life-Elation Force!

Our Spiritual Fractal Formation is in Self-Creation!

Body + Spirit +Mind + Self-Consciousness + Super-Consciousness

= *Holistically Enlightened You!*

Our Personal Gravitational Force is Accumulating Self-Worth!

2. The Philosophy of Permanent Self-Growth

The technological evolution that we are experiencing now has touched upon every corner of the human thought, having shaken the old knowledge and offering *a new, non-stereotyped vision of the world.* So, the means of managing the human psyche must adjust to the present-day demands because tension is the life killer now.

Personal consonance is shaken more than ever!

With all due respects to the wizards of psychotherapy of the previous centuries - *Sigmund Fraud, Carl Yung, Salvador Minchin, Care Whitaker* and others, we have to admit that we are way too different now, and the pivotal question of psychology, "Who are You?" remains unanswered because we can't qualify ourselves in old terms. We need new tools to address our problems and to establish the inner equilibrium at the exponentially changing pace of life. *A stereotyped format of psychotherapy is lagging behind, and it's not time refined.*

It hurts to be human now more than ever!

Most personal breakdowns, alcohol and drug abuses, violence and numerous divorces occur as the means for an individual to tolerate an intolerable situation that a visit to a psychotherapist can hardly help to deal with because there is no system of **SELF-HELP HYPNOTHERAPY.** The idea of the people, mostly young ones, how to help themselves is patriarchal. The lessons of life are not learnt, and ignorance about one's own psychological make-up is appalling.

The technological back-up of life helps us live beyond the survival needs and enriches us with the tools that liberate the body and the mind. Apparently, we must take a much closer look at ourselves and learn the new operative system of **SELF-MANAGEMENT.**

The Life Gains are in the Inwardly Processed Life Pains!

3. Our Time is the Age of New Awareness!

Apparently, we all need a **MANUAL OF LIFE** to go beyond survive! The choice to live as *a free human being,* not indoctrinated by the society, enjoying his / her individuality, realizing the unique potential, and getting self-installed professionally and self-realized personally is a tough choice to make. I think that we can enact the process of self-creation and self-transformation with the help of *autosuggestibility,* or *psychologically charged self-programming* that proves to be extremely affective in terms of improving the *physical, emotional, mental, spiritual, and universal* make-up of a person .

To become spirit-refined, be more life-admiring and self-inspired!

Self-perfection is a lifetime job that is, in fact, *self-consciousness in action,* the consciousness that <u>cultivates a New Culture of thinking, feeling, and living and directs a person</u> to going **beyond the terrestrial boundaries into the unfathomable future!** We can do that by narrowing the boundaries of our ignorance, outlined for us now by the exponentially growing digital technology.

<u>So, what are we supposed to be more aware of ?</u>

1.First, we are immortal beings in **the Field of Universal Consciousness** <u>that we need to be consciously connected to.</u> Each life is part of the universal program, and each one is under its eternal watch.

We are One with everything under the Sun!

2. Our social environment is impacting us negatively without our conscious realization of it. *So, be free to be the best of Thee!*

Be self-governable, not mass media programmable!

3. We forget to be always aware of the direction we are moving to self-worth-wise. Are you moving forward or backward? *Are you standing still and stagnate or self-re-fate?*

4. We need **to constantly grow physically, emotionally, mentally, spiritually ,and universally!** *"The day that you decided that you can't become better, the record of your life starts rolling around the same tune. " (David Bowie)* Drive your life consciously and responsibly!

Your self-worth must be in the constant holistic growth!

5. We need **to beat the indifference in the heart** to always <u>keep it in sync with the mind.</u> The declarations:**" I don't care," "What do I care?" or "I care less!"** should be sent to recess! *Being impersonal is turning you into a characterless human stew!*

6. We need the books at hand and the mind-sets in our smart phones to constantly remind us of **the necessity for self-discipline and self-control,** changing our impulsivity to conscious reasonable thinking.

<u>*Life-Gaining is in Self-Taming!*</u>

7. Every day, week, month, and year, you need to be getting further and further from what you have been so far and start **getting closer to what you are Not, but what you Can be!** Charge yourself with:

I can, I want to…, and I will…!

8. Love yourself and support yourself! Don't expect praises from anyone. Compliment yourself and magnetize your self-worth with more and more self-growth. <u>No fake self-presentation or fake elation!</u>

A smile, the posture, and a good mood are my emotional food!

9. Finally, **coach yourself in the flow of life by the holistic paradigm** *Synthesis-Analysis-Synthesis!* in business, relationships, and self-growth.

Generalize – Internalize - Personalize – Strategize - Actualize!

Synthesis – Analysis -Synthesis!

Every Morning, smile to the Sun that reminds Thee, "Everything I Have, I Do, and I See Gladdens Me!"

4. Self-Consciousness Formation is Our Sole Obligation!

In the book *"Self-Worth,"* I present the ways of the holistic self-worth monitoring through *five stages of self-consciousness development.* On the spiral of self-evolution, it is our main evolutionary goal now, and we need to raise self-consciousness holistically in five dimensions, featured in my five books on *Self-Resurrection* consequentially. *(www.language-fitness.com):*

1) **Mini** - *Physical level –" I Am Free to Be the Best of Me!"(Body)*

2) **Meta** - *Emotional - "Soul-Refining!"(Spirit)*

3) **Mezzo** –*Mental –" Living Intelligence or the Art of Becoming!"(Mind)*

4) **Macro** – *Spiritual - " Self-Taming!" (Self-Consciousness)*

5) **Super** – *Universal -"Beyond the Terrestrial!" (Super Consciousness)*

Universal Intelligence is the conceptual structure of life!

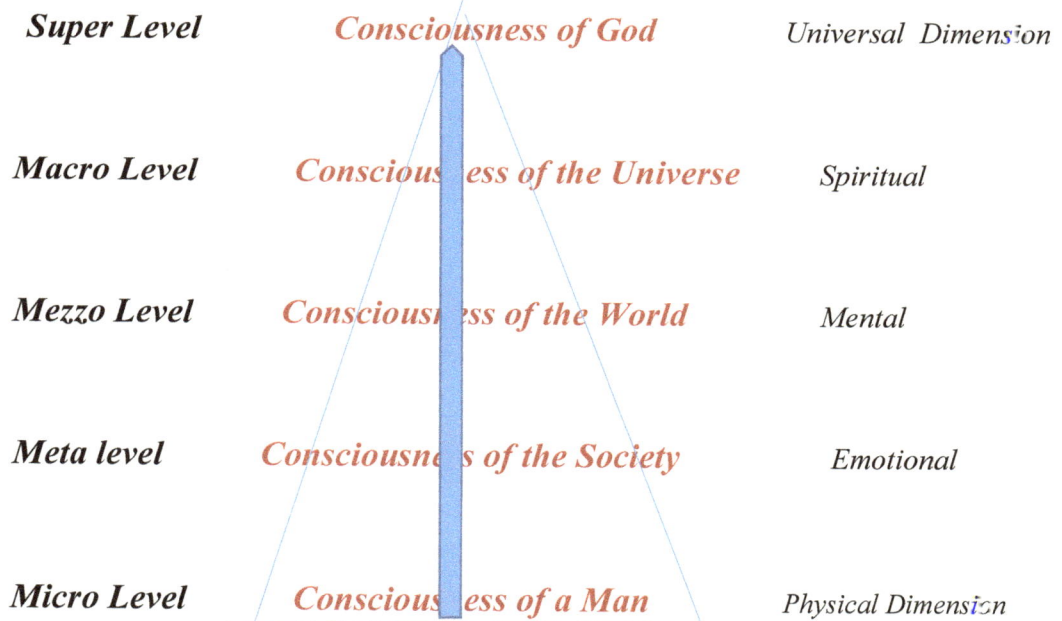

Super Level	Consciousness of God	*Universal Dimension*
Macro Level	*Consciousness of the Universe*	*Spiritual*
Mezzo Level	*Consciousness of the World*	*Mental*
Meta level	*Consciousness of the Society*	*Emotional*
Micro Level	*Consciousness of a Man*	*Physical Dimension*

Our planet is plunging into a new era of consciousness, and our role now is to decipher its new text as the reflection of it in our rising self-consciousness with the help of the new technological tools. .

The Universal Consciousness is ruling the World and You in it, too!

5. The Steps of Realization of Self-Worth on the Planet Earth

The books on self-creation, presented above are comprising the *physical, emotional, mental, spiritual, and universal* levels of life, featuring consequentially <u>five stages</u> of Self-Resurrection and *Self-Worth* accumulation - **Self-Awareness, Self-Monitoring, Self-Installation, Self-Realization,** and **Self-Salvation.** (*See "Living Intelligence or the Art of Becoming! - the Global Book Excellence Award winner /, 2020*

We are developing ourselves moving from one step to the next, getting stuck at any of them, or even getting to the very bottom of the paradigm and starting the journey all over again. The ability to put ourselves together on **the fractal level of spiritual maturation** is our salvation!

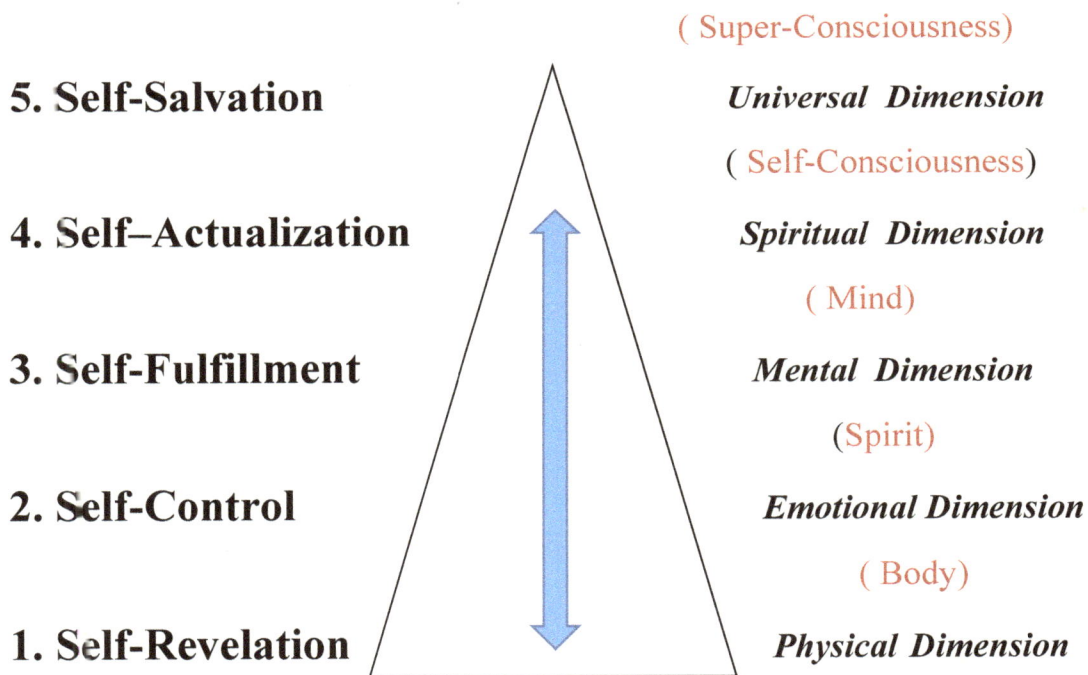

(Super-Consciousness)

5. Self-Salvation   *Universal Dimension*

(Self-Consciousness)

4. Self–Actualization   *Spiritual Dimension*

(Mind)

3. Self-Fulfillment   *Mental Dimension*

(Spirit)

2. Self-Control   *Emotional Dimension*

(Body)

1. Self-Revelation   *Physical Dimension*

The Spiritual Fractal of Being:

Body + spirit + mind + self-consciousness + super-consciousness

Self-Worth Perfection is the Way to Self-Resurrection!

6. Aristocracy of the Spirit

Self-management is, in fact, the work at *the aristocracy of the spirit* that constitutes the best qualities the humanity has developed for the centuries of brutal survival, based on learning life, not just researching it, hoping one day to start it all over again.

The one who stops learning and soul-refining is slowly dying.

There are numerous stories that are reflected in the religious sources, in different fairy tales from all over the world, in ballads, mythology, in the best pieces of literature, music, and art telling us about the beauty of a man's spirit displayed in the most outrageous circumstances. They have become the lessons of strength, tolerance, endurance, love, and *an exceptional nobility of the spirit* that inspires us for generations on end.

The greatest energy remains to be the energy of the unbeatable Spirit of Thee!

"The Best of Me!" spirit constitutes a man's self-worth and is motivating him to grow and develop himself toward full self-realization in life. *Without a deeply rooted sense of self-worth, no one can accomplish much on the planet Earth!* The knowledge of today is outdated tomorrow, and learning is our *Perpetua Mobile* because the quality of life depends on the quality of people living it.

Self-Worth is the motor of Perpetua Mobile on Earth!

Naturally, it's our primary responsibility to perfect ourselves *physically,* establish self-control *emotionally,* enrich ourselves *mentally, ennoble spiritually,* and motivate self-growth *universally.* Such self-growth will enable us to go beyond the habits that limit us and develop the skills that enhance and raise self-consciousness – the common goal of our life on Earth.

Starting at the Universal Bay, Redefine Yourself Every Day!

7. The Methodology of New Unautomated Reflective Thinking

Meanwhile, sameness is what is depleting our lives of their peculiar, individual sense. Apparently, we desperately need **to work at our exceptionality** and *acquire the self-worth of an authentic value* to be able to prove our uniqueness, not common bleakness.

We have a **CELESTIAL OBLIGATION** to become a small, but a very meaningful *beacon of glory, not shame, of the Universe*. It can happen if the majority of us focusses on obtaining personal freedom and accomplishing a higher self-consciousness, following the numerous examples of the most meaningful lives in the history of the humanity. In every book of mine, I keep reminding you to boost your personal uniqueness by constantly instilling   the following auto-induction into the mind:

I am unique in every stance,

I was born, but only once,

There wasn't, there isn't, there won't ever be

Anyone like Me!

The American people are amazingly creative and innovative, being inspired by the freedom of choices that they make and the competition of the ideas that they need to surpass. However, there's one aspect of an American life that mars the exceptionality of the people. A common question" *What's he / she worth?"* is about *the monitory status of a person,* not the richness of his / her inner world, intelligence, and aristocratic values. A money-loaded person is well-respected and highly rated everywhere. His / her self-worth is secondary.

The Money God is Ruling Our Inner World, till What?

8. We're Accumulating the Heights of Self-Worth from Birth!

As is shown above, **the concept of self-worth is holistic in its essence.** It's something that we are working on all our life. Some people are constructing their lives the entire lifetime span, allotted to them from the Above. They die without regrets and the words **"No Regrets"** are even engraved on the gravestones of such people. However, most of people in the world live on the automatic drive, unconsciously destroying themselves in money or fun chasing. They are not aware of the negative vibrations they might be filling their space with. Their self-worth is ,in fact, sheer egoism , negligence , and ignorance.

They have a soul – fungus that's eating them alive from inside.

Self- worth is the result of self-growth! Like money gets accumulated in the bank where we deposit it, self-worth gaining is the process of accumulating good habits and actionable, life-propelling skills. You do not get self-worth from birth; you are developing it consciously all your life. We are not born aristocratic in the heart and mind, we become aristocratic with self-discipline, self-control and conscious self-creation. *Richard Wetherill* offers his recipe of life to us.

"Life is playing out right when it is lived right. Right is Might!"

We are responsible for the feeling of self-worth in ourselves and in our kids. Self-worth is also the method of raising a child by developing his /her skill of scanning oneself **physically, emotionally, mentally, spiritually, and universally.** (*Check out five books on Self-Resurrection*) If you are self-growth oriented, your kids will follow though, learning together with you to take care of the body, emotions, the mind, and **conscience that is our testing device** in raising self-consciousness – our personal way of *proving self-exceptionality.*

Self-Worth Gaining is in Self-Training!

9. The Metamorphosis of Self-Worth Shouldn't Be the Lost Course!

The multi-dimensional holistic vision of life comes with your full awareness of the necessity to form *New Spiritualized Life Fractals* that require the metamorphosis of our old habits and the transformation of self-worth into a new, self-constructive, goal- oriented force.

To be able *to apply the holistic paradigm* presented above to life, we need to have more awareness of life and appreciate its present, or *"to live in the Now" (Eckhart Tolle)* consciously, continuously, and religiously. As *Neale Donald Walsch* puts it,

"When you are in the present, it becomes the present of God!"

Awareness means to be aware of life *"As is"* at this moment without any judgement with full acceptance of the gift of life that yet needs to be unwrapped and appreciated. Freeing the spirit and raising the self-consciousness is everyone's individual responsibility now. It must be instilled in the minds and hearts of our children as early as possible through personality development that we need to sustain as role models. Developing ourselves and our kids in sync , we are learning to live by *mind + heart indivisible unity* that our two inner barometers - *conscience* and *intuition* tune us up to, making our lives godlier, more conscientious, considerate, and full of faith and love.

Unfortunately, the future of our human souls does not seem to be promising in view of the accelerating development of cold, inhuman intelligence that lacks spiritual insightfulness that is our role to breathe into it. Due to high tech explosion, life has a different narrative of the *erosion of self-worth* for those who are not aware of its positive evolutionary transformation. So, let's not blame technology and think of our own eulogy.

Make Your Heart Smart and the Mind Kind! Be One of a Kind!

10. Erosion of Self-Worth

I'd like here to draw the parallel with a wonderful story" *"Metamorphosis"* by a great German writer *Franz Kafka* whose observation of human feelings, inadequacy of behavior, guilt, and isolation can be viewed by us now as **a great warning of the degradation the a man's self-worth** that inevitably brings a person down on the life ladder.

Kafka tells us about a young man, the main character of the story, *Gregor Samsa*, who got transformed overnight into a gigantic cockroach. Naturally, he became an object of disgrace to his family, an outsider in his own home, a quintessentially alienated man. He is appalled at the insignificance of his existence that could hardly be called life. As W. H. Auden writes,*" Kafka is important to us because his predicament is the predicament of a modern man."*

Obviously, when a human being loses his / her self-worth, the degradation of the soul follows because he / she can no longer perform attunement to the **Universal Intelligence - God**. Self-worth is best revealed if you come to God only at the time of need.

But faith must be a permanent wealth!

Only developing our conscious mind in sync with the sub-conscious one, can we raise our super-consciousness that makes it possible **to tune the mind and heart to the Super Mind** that is governing all life in the universe.

When a person knows his / her exceptionality in life, he /she cherishes its value and goes determinedly towards full realization of this exceptionality, his / her dream gets formed into a one-pointed goal in the mind that is pushing you to the stars. **Then self-exceptionality becomes self-realization without vanity.**

Be Self-Refining! Internalize and Eternalize Your Becoming!

11. The Self-Worth Forming Course

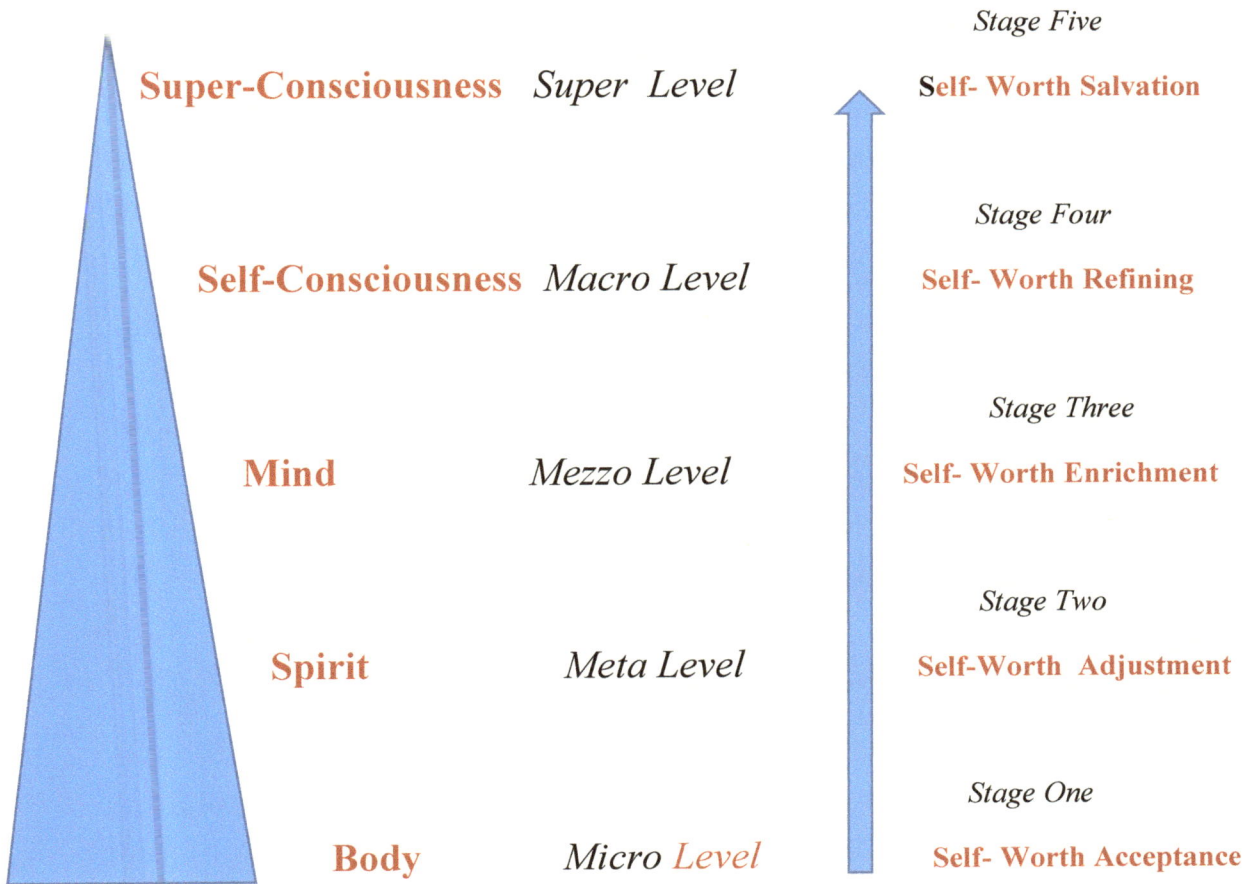

		Stage Five
Super-Consciousness	*Super Level*	**Self- Worth Salvation**
		Stage Four
Self-Consciousness	*Macro Level*	**Self- Worth Refining**
		Stage Three
Mind	*Mezzo Level*	**Self- Worth Enrichment**
		Stage Two
Spirit	*Meta Level*	**Self-Worth Adjustment**
		Stage One
Body	*Micro Level*	**Self- Worth Acceptance**

Let's turn the self-destructive mechanism into self -worth constructive algorithm!

(Body+ Spirit+ Mind) + (Self-Consciousness + Universal Consciousness)

Next, the route of self-worth formation, presented above is featured in *five stages of self-worth formation* in the book. You are invited to do a little scanning of these five most important levels of self-worth, building it up in yourself holistically, *focusing on the Best of You,* level by level and coming up to the top of *Self-Realization* and *Self-Salvation* with a visual back-up in the mind.

Make Your Self-Worth the Main Life Building Force!

12. Only a Personality Can Create A New Self-Worth Reality!

Concluding the introduction to the book, let me reiterate that happiness, in my understanding, is based on self-love that, in turn, is built up by the person's self-worth that allows a person to take the bad with the good of life, without betraying the inner Self.

Both are inseparable with the mental self-enrichment, that, in turn, requires **constant X-raying of bad habits** and transformation of them into **good life-forming skills**. .Such actionable self-worth formation will enthuse your desire for full Self-Realization that, in fact, culminates in S**elf-Salvation,** or a well-lived life. The plan of action is above = <u>Habits + Skills // Heart + Mind / Form + Content</u> of life beyond survive.

> **"If we cannot eliminate the bad in us, we should illuminate the best!"** *(Leo Vygotsky)*

It's the path from common unconsciousness and negativity, from fear and doubt, from discontent and aimlessness, from dispersing of love energy and lack of faith, <u>to conscious</u> **SELF-CONSTRUCTION** in action. You will be discovering your exceptionality, your goal, the call from the Above, and *<u>you'll manage to authenticate your fate!</u>*

Self-discipline is needed to climb the new reality heights *<u>physically, emotionally, mentally, spiritually, and universally.</u>* Doing it, we experience two types of pain –**"either it is the pain from discipline, or the pain from regret."** *(Will Smith)*

What's in it Your Bet?

We're Now in the Robotic State of Self-Consciousness, lacking Self-Worth, Self-Discipline, and Self-Control.

Let's Change its Role!

Stage One

(The Physical Level of Self-Scanning)

Self-Worth
Acceptance

"Self-acceptance is more important than self-improvement"

(Dr. Paul Pearsall)

Self-Worth is Me; Self-Worth is My Philosophy!

Our Salvation is in the Inner Self-Emancipation!

Life-Elation is in Ascending the Skies of Self-Creation!

The Thrill of the Lifetime is in Sky Diving!

1. To Get to Know Your Inner Self, Look Inside Yourself!

(Physically, emotionally, mentally, spiritually, and universally)

Be an Objective
Self-Worth Judge,
Don't Just -
Self-Oblige!

Overcoming laziness is the first step to accumulating worthiness and characterful-ness!

Start with overpowering the lazy spell, "I don't want to do it!" or "I hate to do it!" with commanding to your inner array,

"Do it, anyway!"

Be a Human Being - a Miracle of Self-Seeing!

Self-Induction :

To Build up Your Personal Fort, Master the Inner World!

2. Self-Love is a Fragile Stuff!

The world is full of unhappy people who want to satisfy their internal hunger for **self-love, self-development, self-adjustment, self-realization, and self-salvation**, but they do not know how to attain that.

Evolution has awarded us with the main gift - Consciousness!

Therefore, it's essential for us to expand our awareness of life and find our unique place in it. Every person has **an information etalon** in his / her DNA, and <u>if a man's inner informational field is identical to this etalon,</u> the man enjoys harmony and calmness in life. But if there is a deviation from **the DNA etalon,** a man suffers from discomfort, depression, and discontent because his cells go havoc unsupervised.

Aware attention to life and living is a must! "Right is Might!"

By the same token, a person wouldn't improve himself, unless he has the reason to love himself and respect himself for something he has done or is doing. Then, self-respect is getting transformed into self-confidence, and self-love gets deeply rooted in the person's soul. Most importantly, such **consolidation of self-worth** should not be based or should not depend on anyone's approval. Induct yourself with,

I don't compete or compare; I'm just the best here and there!

People vary in their intelligence, values, levels of compassion and self-consciousness, and if such levels are not high enough, a person on whose opinion you might rely or whose approval you might be seeking only ruins your self-esteem. The auto-induction below needs to be at the core of your forming self-worth because **the image of a self- worth-oriented personality** is in your own life quest, not anyone's.

<u>In my Life Quest, I am the Best!</u>

Look at the best leaders in the history of the humanity. They were unshakable in their self-belief, and no one could ever change the route that they had chosen to complete their **unique mission on earth.**

"My Life is My Mission!" (Gandhi)

3. A New Level of Life Awareness

We live at the time of a new level of awareness .*Dr. Bruce Lipton* , a digital biologist, calls this **new level of awareness** about our biological and mental make-up *"informational medicine."* He suggests we learn to transform ourselves to better, younger, and healthier people **by re-programming our cells.** They need a good, mindful, and well-informed manager.

 Our digitally educated idea of ourselves demands we change the limited view that we are victims of a hereditary DNA. *Dr. Lipton* believes that genes are not responsible for our personalities**, but our programming of ourselves through our cells is**. My understanding of the Self-Worth formation, therefore, goes beyond the accepted view that the personality traits are a given.

You can **form your spiritual fractal** *(See above)* by governing yourself through five holistic stages of living - from **_physical_** fitness to **_emotional_** control. Next, you need to focus on **_mental_** clarity, **_spiritual_** transformation, and **_universal_** unification. Thus, you'll gradually get to grips with a new way of thinking, feeling, and acting, and you'll start climbing new heights of your living and being.

You'll stop crawling and start flying, like a caterpillar that gets transformed into a butterfly.

Be sure to have a new **SELF-WORTH IMAGE,** instilled in your mind as the blueprint for self-transformation by the mind-set:

I Can…! I want to…! , and I will…!

Don't let your imagination limit you in your dreams, plans, and. ideas. Believe in them, but do not share them with anyone. *We profess, but God provides!* Indeed, if you work on your transformation consciously, you'll evolve together with the Universe and the planet Earth!

Inspirational Auto-Induction is the Onto-Genesis of Self-Production!

4. The Auto-Suggestive Meditation for Self-Worth Rejuvenation!

Accumulating Self-Worth is directly connected with meditation and *Inspirational Auto-Suggestive* **SELF-ECOLOGY** when every chunk of information and plenty mind-sets, illustrating the concepts below can be used for <u>programming your cells, your minicomputers</u>, in the way you want yourself to develop in all five dimensions.

Life-refining is in self-programming!

Sit comfortably in the armchair, or on the bench outside, close your eyes and start <u>inducting your cells with the **BEST IMAGE** of yourself</u>. Visualize yourself at the time that you liked yourself most and you felt happy and hopeful. See yourself with those beautiful, shiny eyes, great hair, shapely body, and a broad happy smile on the face. <u>Declare out loud and induct your cells with the following mind-set;</u>

"I'm transforming myself into the being with a new thinking, feeling and seeing! From this time on, I'll be getting younger, healthier, and happier with every minute, hour, or a day. That's my everyday say!"

Let the state of rejuvenation permeate the whole of you, every cell of you. To literally experience this state, practice <u>breathing through your skin, head, hair, the palms of your hands, your organs</u> *(liver, pancreas, kidney, stomach, the gut),* the pelvic area, the legs, and the souls of your feet. <u>Breathing in,</u> *induct the first part of any of the mind-sets you might resonate to in this book,* <u>breathing out,</u> *say inwardly the second part of it.* You are the President of your cells. Talk them into following you, *"I'm my best friend* (breathe in)*; I'm my beginning and my end!"* (out)

Youth, grace, and health (breathe in) *are my inner wealth!* (breathe out)

Visualize your cells, feel them, and call on them to become eternally young and beautiful, <u>transforming you into a new state of light and love.</u> When you are outside, say *Hello"* to the four elements of life – *the Sun* (fire)*, the Air , the Earth, and the Ocean.*(the water) Thank the energy of the Universe for helping you transform your whole being.

into *a younger, self-worth - unified state of a New You!* Get *physically, emotionally ,mentally, spiritually, and universally connected* to **the Master Mind in you** and everywhere! This auto-suggestive meditation, even if casually done, will help you <u>radiate light from inside, illuminating the darkness of the bad habits</u> and magnetizing new good skills. Most importantly, it will fortify the skill of working at your self-transformation holistically! As a result, people will start gravitating to your <u>fractal wholeness</u>.

(Body+ Spirit+ Mind) + (Self-Consciousness + Universal Consciousness)

"Like electricity needs to be wired correctly, our souls need to be wired to our consciousness."(Nikola Tesla) and together they get connected to the *Universal Field of Consciousness. (Dr. John Hagelin)*

Right now, **we are mostly driven by a compulsive behavior and demands of the body,** forgetting about <u>the other ingredients of the human fractal</u> that we are supposed to form inside to become truly self-conscious and mentally connected to the Universal Informational Field. Only such connection provides us with **a new worldview** and gives us much food for thought that can transform the self-worth of those who learn to digest it and use it constructively to change themselves and the world around them. <u>There are no shortcuts in achieving this transformation</u> because **"the hardest job to do is the job at oneself!** *(Dalai Lama)*You must be willing to do it by stretching the mind's outfit, **working meditatively at re-programming your body's cells** and <u>enlarging spiritually the volume of your soul!</u>

We need to change the" izm" of the self- development algorism!

Then, our world will have no racism or any skin color discrimination, no national fights, superiority complexes, based on people's financial status, no moral degradation, just evolution without frustration!

<u>*New, spiritualized intelligence = new quality people!*</u>

I Wish I Could Live then, in the Unanswerable When?!

5. Change Your Life's Algorithm to Self-Enthusiasm!

Our goal in life now is *to change our perception of the local reality to the absolute reality!* It means that we need to learn to materialize a constructive, creative, moral, inspirational, and love-oriented reality that would make us happy not de juror, but de facto.

Let's change the lenses through which we see the world!

The possibilities of the brain are limitless, and we just need to induct our minds with the consistently recurrent constructive thoughts and feelings that will form new neurological circuits and re-shape our past for good.

The most crucial thing is to learn *not to make the same habitual, predictable decisions* that were determining our behavior yesterday. Don't be limited to the wishes of the body!

Living is being new every day! A new day is a new say!

People often complain that they can forgive, but they cannot forget. That's only natural because everything is stored in the subconscious mind, our computer drive. So, to be emotionally fit, don't activate the past without any need. Focus on love and loving! Only love determines our self-worth that keeps us remembered on Earth!

Learn to inwardly celebrate the chosen fate!

If life were going the way it was planned , it would be truly boring. We live in the world of energy and intelligence, and the fluctuations that life is based on are still not quite qualified in quantum physics. But one thing is irrefutable - *change is the trajectory of your life.*

Living is fun, but it must be consciously done!

Life Literacy Must be Devoid of Stagnation and Obstinacy!

6. The Self-Worth Formation is in Selection and Self-Organization

Constructive self-change is a voluntary thing. Nevertheless, self-change may turn out to be impossible after a certain age of a person. when his / her bad habits are so deeply engraved in the mind that it gets disconnected with the heart permanently. The person becomes barren for self-analysis or any self-reconstruction.

" That which is crooked cannot be made straight." (Ecclesiastes, 15)

1) The decision to change the flow of things from the negative vector to the positive one is the first crucial step to make. You need to go through the process of **SELECTION** of the people around you, the habits you have, the job that you do, the friends that roam around, the relationships, and the funds available to count on.

This selection process must be carried out consciously in five-dimensions - physical, emotional, mental, spiritual and universal.

Everything and everyone that might be in the way of *a holistic make-over* must be rid of. The pyramid of qualities in five dimensions that you need to process your self-worth through is presented in the next chunk of information. Such **SELF-SCANNING** must also be objective and without anyone's opinion to be considered. *Give your conscience a rest with an honesty test!*

Life-gaining is in self-taming!

2) SELF-ORGANIZATION is the next action in self-worth formation. It will require sifting of the redundant information in the mind and *getting rid of the chaos* in the thoughts, emotions and random, impulsive actions that result into *"vanity and vexation of spirit."* (Ecclesiastes, 1)

It means that you should not shorten the lifetime span, allotted to you from the Above with fun-chasing and an irrational, automatic lifestyle, casual relationships, and aimless killing of time.

With ***the blueprint of Self-Resurrection*** instilled in your mind, try to organize your life in five holistic stages, presented in this book. Channel your life through these stages ***holistically,*** not separating one stage from the next in your self-perception and self-scanning.

Self-Awareness + Self-Monitoring + Self-Installation + Self-Realization + Self-Salvation

3) SELF-TRANSFORMATION (*Re-formation)* is the third action to consider. It means that we should not speed up or shorten your lifetime span with fun-chasing and an irrational, automatic lifestyle, but you need to consciously focus on making much more difference in life and justifying your self-worth to yourself and the world.

The inner dignity of the whole is the aristocratism of your soul!

The actionable work on: ***Selection + Organization + Self-Transformation*** will harmonize your soul. Your mind will get back to order, helping you establish self-content, calmness, and inner equilibrium. You'll get to know and love yourself more and eventually, work out your own **HAPPINESS ALGORYTHM**, based on the blueprint of Self Resurrection, channeling your self-worth in *the physical, emotional, mental, spiritual, and universal dimensions* consequentially and consciously according to your own vision.

" Be conscious. Consciousness mobilizes!"

(Neale Donald Walsch)

The best power to attain is the power over yourself!

"The hardest job on earth is to be a good person!" (Bernard Show)

Self-Worth Must Be Your Inner Boss!

7. Self-Ecology Pyramid

I write about the necessity of forming the holistic ***"The Best of Me!* self-image** in the book" ***I'm Free to be the Best of Me*!** I present in it the grid of some <u>major self-constructive personality traits</u> in five dimensions. So, the chart below will help you identify which strengths you can link your personality to, building up your self-worth and *what you lack for your self-transformation.* The <u>*selection + organization*</u> action is, in fact, **SELF-SCANNING** that you must conduct **OBJECTIVELY,** revealing ***what you are and what you are Not!***

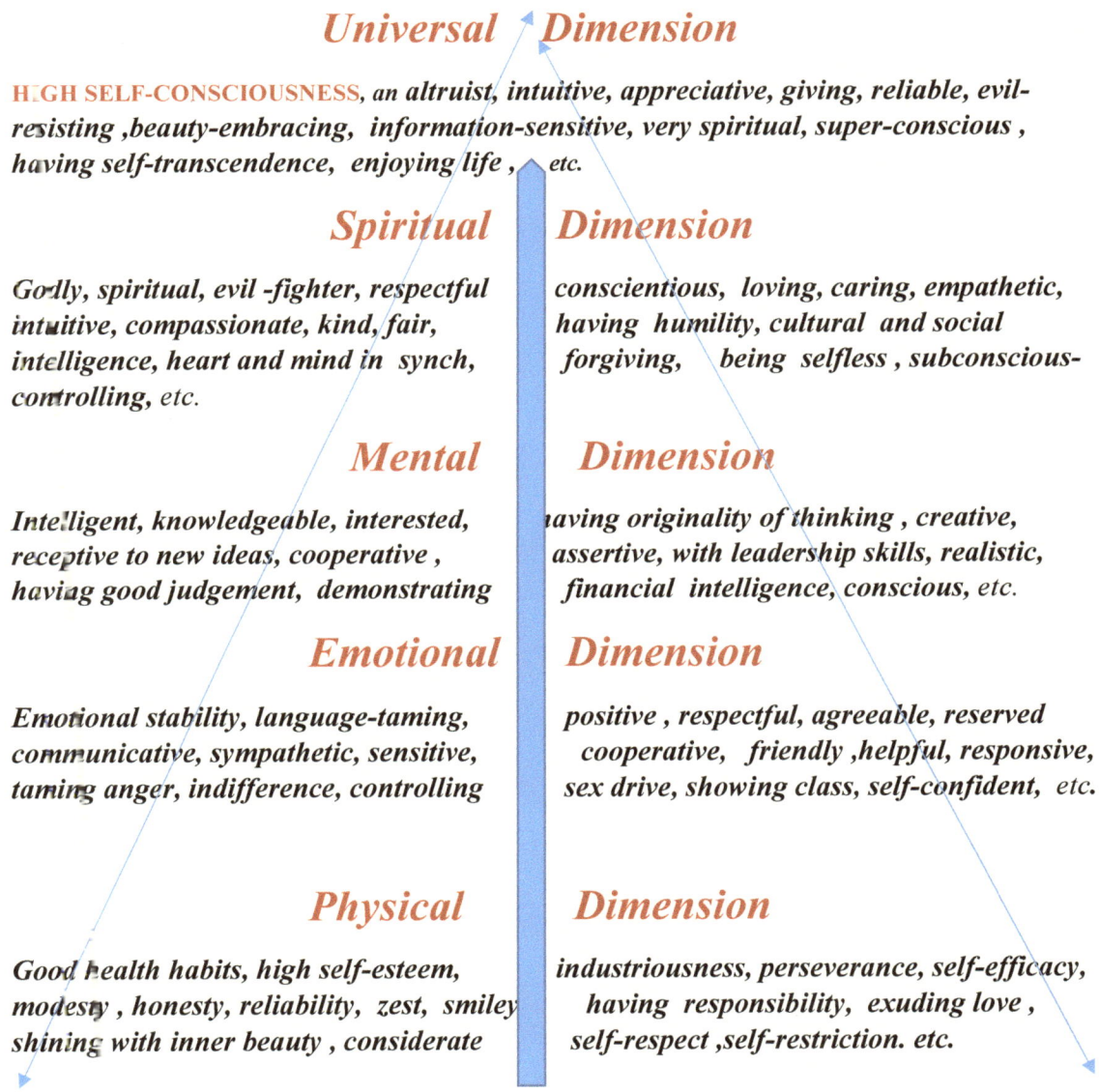

Universal ↑ *Dimension*

HIGH SELF-CONSCIOUSNESS, *an altruist, intuitive, appreciative, giving, reliable, evil-resisting ,beauty-embracing, information-sensitive, very spiritual, super-conscious , having self-transcendence, enjoying life ,* etc.

Spiritual | *Dimension*

Godly, spiritual, evil -fighter, respectful intuitive, compassionate, kind, fair, intelligence, heart and mind in synch, controlling, etc.

conscientious, loving, caring, empathetic, having humility, cultural and social forgiving, being selfless , subconscious-

Mental | *Dimension*

Intelligent, knowledgeable, interested, receptive to new ideas, cooperative , having good judgement, demonstrating

having originality of thinking , creative, assertive, with leadership skills, realistic, financial intelligence, conscious, etc.

Emotional | *Dimension*

Emotional stability, language-taming, communicative, sympathetic, sensitive, taming anger, indifference, controlling

positive , respectful, agreeable, reserved cooperative, friendly ,helpful, responsive, sex drive, showing class, self-confident, etc.

Physical | *Dimension*

Good health habits, high self-esteem, modesty , honesty, reliability, zest, smiley shining with inner beauty , considerate

industriousness, perseverance, self-efficacy, having responsibility, exuding love , self-respect ,self-restriction. etc.

I Am the Whole Me; I am the Best I Could Ever Be!

8. The Realization of Self-Worth on the Planet Earth!

Summing the concepts above, we should be developing ourselves consequentially in *five stages of Self-Resurrection*, easily visualized and imprinted in the mind as: *Self-Awareness, Self- Monitoring, Self-Installation, Self-Realization,* and *Self-Salvation.*

Self-growth **is to be monitored from one stage to the next, getting stuck at any of them, or even getting** to the very bottom of the pyramid and performing **SELF-ECOLOGY** all over again. The ability to put ourselves together in the *fractal level formation of spiritual maturation is our salvation*.

Body + Spirit + Mind + Self-Consciousness + Super-Consciousness

= *Self-Resurrection* (See www.language-fitness.com / section *Self-Resurrection*)

Stages of Self-Growth: (**Super-Consciousness**)

5. **Self-Salvation**   *Universal Dimension*

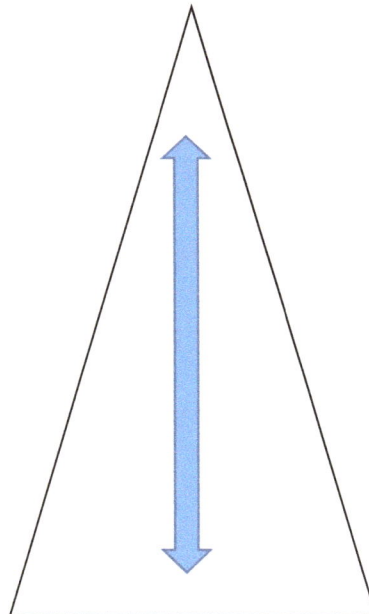

(**Self-Consciousness**)

4. **Self-Realization**   *Spiritual Dimension*

(**Mind**)

3. **Self-Fulfillment**   *Mental Dimension*

(**Spirit**)

2. **Self-Control**   *Emotional Dimension*

(**Body**)

1. **Self-Revelation**   *Physical Dimension*

"Man chooses to corrupt due to a lack of awareness and inability to love God within himself." (John Baines)

Self-Worth Perfection is the Way to Self-Resurrection!

9. Tame Your Analytical Thinking to Give a Chance to Visual Inking!

It is pointless, however, to talk about self-resurrection if you didn't consciously realize who you are and what your self-worth is, <u>not in monetary terms</u>, but viewed *in time* (your limited life) *and space* (the place you are in on the planet Earth).

I'm trying with this book to pinpoint the ways of performing self-change and self-growth, not as a dictator or a psycho-analysist, but as a friend who has been on this path herself and who has put on it hundreds of her students from different countries of the world, having inspired them to transform themselves with <u>the vision of much higher standards of themselves instilled in their minds.</u>

Our brain has an amazing skill - it can *filter the information* that it recognizes from the one it doesn't. It is called *the vermicular actualizing system* that, unfortunately, works not in our favor. The brain is ready to discern and process the information that you always agree with without any effort. It does it by force of habit that had been formed from birth. <u>It's a support system against the revolting thoughts,</u> trying to baffle the brain with unpredictable solutions.

To enrich self-worth in every cell , transcend yourself!

So, to direct the brain toward self-change, you need to re-program it for *the new habits + skills unity* or change **the form** and **the content** of your life and thus, generate a holistic **SELF-WORTH SYSTEM.**

Form + Content of the human essence in twine form a New Life Paradigm!

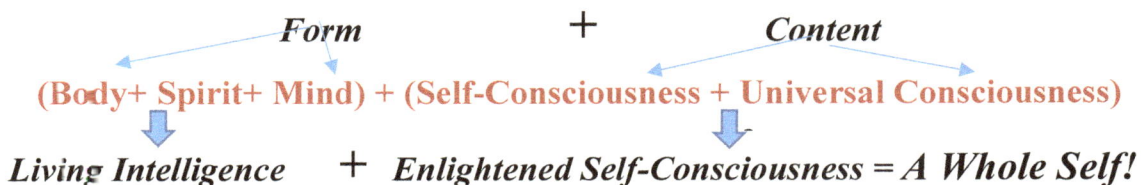

Form + *Content*

(Body+ Spirit+ Mind) + (Self-Consciousness + Universal Consciousness)

Living Intelligence + *Enlightened Self-Consciousness = A Whole Self!*

To Self-Rein, Generate a New Self-Worth System in the Brain!

10. Keep Your Soul in the Holistically Monitored Self-Control!

Mass media is constantly programming us with skepticism, blunt jokes, heartless reactions to our falls and failures, with sticking labels and laughing at our sincere openness about something that was not up-the par on the society's scale of values.

Build up immunity to the socially polluted insecurity!

If we follow suit, we get in the bad habit of fake laughing and exaggerated elation, of fun seeking and superficial judgements .

Being fake is building a twisted fate!

As the result of being in the cyber space of someone's twisted reality, we become *de-magnetized and petty-wise.* We listen to someone's advice and give ours, not giving a damn how it will work out.

Life takes a backward course of degrading the self-worth!

Fear and doubt penetrate our inner cyber space and corrode our souls, *destroying the* **HEART+ MIND** *link that must be in sync!* It's vital to be vigilant and never stop listening to your **INTUITION CONTROL DEVICE** which is very wise. *Edgar Cayce* suggesting commanding to oneself in such situations," **HALT!"** It really works.

Also, try to get into the habit of scanning your self-worth and establishing a vigilant control over your *physical, emotional, mental, spiritual, and universal domains* every day when you go to bed and scan your accomplishments / failures during that day.

Remember that the necessity to monitor your bad habits never becomes irrelevant. So, in every book, I keep reminding you of an excellent statement made by *Albert Einstein,*

"Bad habits have a good tendency — either you kill them, or they kill you."

11. Launch Yourself to the Universal Life Energy Spell!

To launch yourself to action when a problem hits is a challenge that depletes us of energy and **weakens the spirit** that is <u>the most vital connecting part in the spiritual fractal formation</u> that is the goal of your life, keeping the form and content of your being in sync. *(See above)*

We cannot affect the circumstances that are beyond our control, but we can change the perception of them and our reaction to them.

It's important not to live inside the problem and allow yourself swim in it for a whole day. Dismiss it, thinking about the vibrational cycle of your heartbeat-*21-21-21— Calm-down, calm-down, calm-down.*

Accept the Rolla Costa rhythm of life and help it with the next up-loading of your spirit's might. Turn your disappointment, distress, insult, fear, <u>depression into life-obsession</u> by turning on your confidence to discover the possibilities that this problem hides.

The problem loses its power over you and you can resolve it .too.

The sense of self-worth will fortify your life's force and wouldn't let you become lethargic, if you constantly scan it in five levels holistically. Such daily X-raying of your *physical state*, *emotional diplomacy* skills, *mental* enrichment, *spiritual* consistence and *universally* unshakable going toward the goal beyond any obstacles strengthens your spirit and the degree of your self-worth value.

The greatest spirit remains to be the spirit of the unbeatable Me!

Remember, **your spiritual awakening** is an everyday job, and your thoughts are just the accumulation of the information that you have gathered so far. So, sift the information you get for its validity.

Every Move is a Chore of Your Space-Time Life Score!

12. Self-Growth Agenda Must Be Unique - Not Bleak!

The lives of the best of us, with **Steve Jobs** as our contemporary being at the of the list, proves that we need to surpass ourselves in being and doing the best we can because there are no limits to perfection.

> *" It's not enough to be the Best; Be the Only!"* (Steve Jobs)

Like the **Golden Ratio** that is discovered to be in the center of the best works of art and architecture and that has a limitless string of numbers going into the infinity, our abilities are limitless,

Break your habitual spell! Get more of yourself!

You can always get more of yourself if you instill in your inner core the belief that you are not just of many, " **you are the Only!"** Obviously, _Steve Jobs never betrayed his self-worth , and he never doubted that it was worth all the troubles, problems, betrayals, and fights to prove to the world that he was the Only!

Your self-worth will always engrave obstacles on your path. There will be enemies and a lot of envy on the part of the people who cannot surpass the crowd mentality and themselves . Be proud of having them, and see the troubles, the foes, and the sarcastic people that rain on your parade as a great accomplishment in life. *Charles Mackay wrote,*

" You have no enemies you say;

Alas, my friend, the boast is poor!

He, who has mingled in the fray of duty

That the brave endure, must have made foes!

If you have none, small is the work that you have done!

Break Your Cell; Surpass Yourself!

13, I'm My Best Friend; I'm My Beginning and My End!

If You Live in the Sun,

No one can do you any Harm!

So, Be in Unity

With your Inner Divinity!

Inner divinity means conscious living and learning. " It is <u>everyday self-scanning through the grid of urgency</u> that helps retain your personal magnetism in any life circumstances."(Eisenhower)

Remember, **personal charisma is not a God-given exceptional quality** that crowns the most successful people and good money-makers .

It's the result of a <u>goal-oriented, self-disciplined, and constantly self-magnetized spirit</u> , and the people who charge it on a regular basis , **don't let anyone or anything demagnetize it in any of the five levels of life**!

"Be a thing in itself!" (Hegel) **Be your own self-reliant Self!**

Spiritual maturation is attained on the path of Self-Realization!

Give Yourself a Chance to Happen!

14. Your Name is the Passport of Your Self-Worth!

Your name is your first personal ID, and to be a proud owner of it is your duty. We do not choose our names , but we must justify them as exceptional even though they might be most common and easily recognizable. Your name may be **Mary or John**, but you must perceive yourself as unique and <u>define your name with your character, morals, manners</u> , and *exceptional personal magnetism* that makes your name stand out in the line of many other same names.

The content that you put in your name defines your self-worth!

As a college professor, I don't find it acceptable for the students to call their professors by their first manes as is the case in the USA. There should be *a functional barrier* between you and the students , you and your employees, you and the people that you just met at any social gathering. <u>The honor of using the first name</u> should be given only to the people that you respect and perceive to be at the same professional and educational level with you. The privilege of using the diminutives should be given only to the loved ones , close friends, and the associates working at the same project with you to remove the obstacles of autocracy. Familiarity is killing a person's self-worth.

Indeed, there's a big difference in *self-worth formation* between being called and perceived *as Larry or Laurence, Billy or William, Jennifer or Jen*. Being on a familiar basis with a person that you hardly know diminishes your self-perception . Other than that, it demagnetizes the **SELF-GRAVITY** of your *personal solar system.* I suggest you instill in your mind a small verse as the self-worth enhancing mind-set:

I'm John / Mary / etc. - One of a Kind

In the Name and the Mind!

There Wasn't, there Isn't, there Won't Ever Be Anyone Like Me!

15. To Become the Most Fulfilled and Loving Self, Be Yourself!

Next, scanning yourself continuously <u>in the physical dimension,</u> being **AUTHENTIC** is the most challenging state of self-worth formation because it requires a lot of self-education, much sorting out of the redundant information and an individual structuring of the brain, *with the left and right hemispheres gradually coming in sync.* Your self-worth is based on the **SELF-GRAVITY** that is formed by the whole brain action that, in turn, <u>magnetizes your personal solar system.</u> The shinier the system, the more people gravitate to your ideas, becoming your co-thinkers and co-creators, or your foes and opposers.

We need to operate against self-perpetuity rate!

To attain mastery over your own life and the lives of other people, you must change the nature of your thoughts and actions, <u>working on self-worth holistically.</u> It means that you must take care of your **physical state** (*weight, strength, beauty*), **emotional self-control** (*emotional diplomacy*), **intellectual broadness** (*professional intelligence*), **spiritual values** (*morals and virtues*) , and **universal aspirations** (*dedication to your dream*). You need to work further on self-perfection in five philosophical levels*: mini, meta, mezzo, macro, and super.*

Science proves that our chromosomes have a *holographic structure which has an electro-magnetic informational field*. It contains the information about the past, present and the future in every genome. The molecules of DNA exchange this information with the help of the electro-magnetic fields around them. Our charging these fields with negative energy resonates negatively in the whole body. The rule here is: *Think what you are thinking!* For the new times to survive,

We need to acquire a New Culture of Life!

Before Saying, "I Can Do It," You Need to Know How to Do It!

16. The Cyber Security of Your Space and Time Unity

I'm sure you will agree with the statement that people admire the "*success dogs,*" but they often follow the *underdogs*. **Comparison is killing people with envy and jealousy.** Unfortunately, **SELF-EROSION** that inevitably leads to *self-worth corrosion* starts with the physical level of our existence. It starts with our early childhood. Disadvantaged kids are those that start suffering from *soul erosion.* Their souls are deeply hurt, abused with tongue-lashing, violence, abandonment, bullying, and now with the **cyber intrusion,** bothering both generations.

Soul - erosion leads to soul corrosion!

Our <u>self-worth formation is a deeply psychological factor</u> that needs to be addressed in schools with the knowledge of the basics of psychology and the values of the **ARISTOCRATISM** of manners and behavior.

Self-worth must be raised from birth!

As I have noted above, *self- worth is a holistic concept* that needs to be questioned daily in the *physical, emotional, mental, spiritual, and universal cyber space*. <u>The avalanche of redundant information, messy phone calls, and impersonal intrusion into our *space - time security*</u> is becoming a real menace for our self-worth formation. So, sort out the people that you allow into your life. <u>Do not let random people into your cyber space, either.!</u> *Scan them in five dimensions for the viruses* that they might transmit to you , or to your kids with their *skepticism, pessimism, racism, or Self-ism.* We need to have the **SCREEN OF PROTECTION** against negative vibes in the social space, especially against *the mass media stereotyped reactions,* indoctrinating our behavior through stupid commercials.

Establish the Vigilant Cyber Control over Your Infinite Soul!

17. Self-Ecology Must Become Your Personal Psychology!

I have mentioned above that **there is no self-worth gravity without intellectual and emotional SANITY.** By sanity, I mean here our constant growing in the *physical, emotional, mental, spiritual, and universal vistas of life, **objectively**,* assessing self-growth in these dimensions and relying on the accumulation of self-worth on this path.

Life is a constructive process , not a fun-chasing result!

Self-sanity is the ability of a person to scan himself objectively, protecting himself from <u>stagnant stereotyped thinking, feeling and acting</u> that deplete one of self-worth and lower it to the common level of automatized or robotized life perception.

Your unique being is in forward seeing!

Of course, Ego remains, but it should not get stale, stubborn, and arrogant! **The self-worth of the people that are too conceited never blossoms!** Blossoming is possible only for the people that can shine from inside with the ability to give, to create, to change the world's fate! People that stop growing, stop living!

Stagnation in force is the death of Self-Worth!

If we stagnate in our old habits, we become hostages of our subconscious mind. Consequently, we are in constant discontent with life that we are not managing in the positive direction, being also intolerant and irritably sarcastic of any progressive changes in others. So, g*ive everyone space and time to stop faking their life and start living it*.

If your help is needed and asked for, be sure to grant it. Trust people and trust yourself! **Have your own Say! Stay away from the people in the stagnation bay!**

Stagnation Vaporizes Us of the Spirit that Makes Self-Worth People Infinite!

18. Keep Your Soul in the Holistically Monitored Self-Control!

Mass media is constantly programming us with skepticism, blunt jokes, heartless reactions to our falls and failures, giving labels and laughing at our sincere openness about something that was not up-the par on the society's scale of values. People judge, not self-worth oblige.

Build up immunity to the socially polluted insecurity!

If we follow suit, we'll get in a bad habit of *fake laughing* and *exaggerated elation*, of fun seeking and superficial, judgements. *To be fake means to be is building a twisted fate!*

As the result of being in the cyber or personal space of someone's twisted reality, we become *de-magnetized and petty-wise.* We listen to someone's advice and give ours, not giving a damn how it'll work out.

Life takes a backward course of degrading the self-worth!

Fear and doubt penetrate our inner cyber space and corrode our souls, destroying the **HEART+ MIND** link that must be in sync! It's vital to be vigilant and *listen to your intuition control device* to be wise.

"Resist, reject, reform your inner de-form!" (Ravi P.S. Berg)

Continue X-raying your self-worth in *the physical, emotional, mental, spiritual, and universal domains* during the day, too. Do it reflectively if you have a problem or any trouble. *Resist, reject, and reform your bad habit to think, feel, and act compulsively.*

Remember that the necessity to monitor your bad habits never becomes irrelevant. Always, keep reminding yourself of Einstein's words. " *Bad habits have a good tendency – either you kill them, or they kill you.* " It takes only a stroke to change a minus into a plus! Do it, thus!

To Retain Your Unique Form, Create the Self-Protective Uniform!

19. Indifference and Impersonality are the Products of Self-Vanity!

The sense of self-worth is also directly connected to a person's **professional intelligence** because while working, *we display our physical fitness, emotional control, **mental** richness, **spiritual** authenticity, and the **universal** dreams* about how to contribute our own bit to the universal outfit. However, we often display too much **inner impersonality and indifference**.*(See the book "Self-Taming")*

The phrases "What do I care? I care less!" create the mess!

Our jobs often dictate a politically correct attitude that is autocratically worded out, prohibiting the employees to go beyond the prescribed rules for fear of losing the life-sustaining job. So, the cases that need more personal, or individualized consideration in resolving any problem that a client might face are treated in *the disconnection of the* **heart + mind link.** Such situations *diminish the self-worth* of both the seller and the buyer, and, most significantly, damage the value of the product or any help that might be needed. The Americans are a great nation of givers, and impersonality shouldn't be an enigma.

"I don't care about your problems. I have mine to consider."

Also**, the feelings of false superiority** generate indifference and apathy, both personally and professionally. We need to make things simpler and much friendlier to people around, not in a fake smiling way, but with the readiness in the heart and mind to help . I'm very thankful to my mother who kept teaching me, a young, inexperienced girl, *" Never turn away from the problems of other people. If you can help, do it!"* The warmth of self-worth that people of the medical professions embrace us with should be the norm in any profession. *"Being kind is much more important than being smart!"* *(Jack Ma)*

"Treat others as you want to be treated!" Must be Studied and Repeated!

20. Be Your Own Best Friend!

Concluding the physical level of self-worth accumulation, it is always a good idea to summarize the work done and to assess the progress of your inner work and self-modification in the most positive way.

There are many very persuasive auto-inductions on the pages of this book They are provided at every level of your self-programming that is meant to up-grade your sense of self -worth and uniqueness

Only he who holds his head can go ahead!

Every one of us needs a mental, emotional, physical, and psychological support - *the support of self-respect and self-modification*. We all get constantly criticized by our parents, the loved ones, friends, bosses, and the people who know nothing about us, but who judge us, anyway, and who give us grades for our looks, manners, speaking, working, and just being everywhere.

There is only one person who always supports us, backs us up in trouble, justifies us for the mistakes we make, understands us like no one else, and who feels pain when we cry and joy when we are happy. This person is you! So, induct your cells with the mind-set below. It's end is at the bottom.

I'm my best friend; I'm my Beginning and my End!

Only you know how great you and what your exceptionality is! Only you feel the need for love and the sense of responsibility for yourself. Only you know deep inside how very special you are, and you can be! You do not want to be a clone of anyone. *You are quite happy with who and what you are!*

You are on the way to your full Self-Realization bay!

Self-Induction:

If Anyone Doesn't Like Me, It's His or Her Problem, not Mine!

21. So, Manage Yourself by Re-Programming Your Cells!

I manage myself

By re-programming my cells!

        I sow into my inner core

        What I want to restore!

I change my spine's feelings

To remain upright in my dealings.

        A smile, the posture , and a good mood

        Are my best spirit's food.

My spirit gets strong and unbeatable

If my cells are programmed and evil impenetrable!

        If my energy is remitted,

        And the outer negative influence is deleted!

Thus, I govern my body's health

And remain the master of my mind's wealth!

        I don't let down my self-guard,

        I keep Angels at my side!

With the reference point of Christ's piercing eyes,

I keep monitoring my self-taming device!

Upload your smart phone with a new Self-Taming tone!
(See "Self-Taming" - HYPERLINK
www.language-fitness.com / video section Self-Resurrection)

I'm Generating a *New Life Symmetry* in Me! I'm a New Me!

Stage Two

(The Emotional Level of Self-Scanning)

Self-Worth

Adjustment

(Self-Worth requires the <u>Heart + Mind</u> sync; Feel but Think!)

"Your life is the expression of your mind's programs because 95% of your life comes from your subconscious. But your goal is <u>to make your conscious mind hold the programs</u> that match your wishes, desires, and aspirations".

(Dr. Bruce Lipton)

Self-Consciousness is a Mile of Life.
Live Consciously; Don't just Survive!

Build Your Emotional Stuff on Authentic Love!

(Etienne Pirot)

Love is Me; Love is My Philosophy!

Your Self-Worth Needs Emotional Control to Be Enforced!

Life Needs to Be Renewed, ## Not Endured!

Be sure not to betray your self-worth array!

X-ray yourself regularly in the emotional level of your holistic life's force!

To get the emotional equilibrium rewards, remove the conflict in your thoughts!

Develop Inner Grace at Your Own Pace!

It is not What God Tells You, ## It's What You Hear!

1. Being Starstruck is a Special Personality Mark!

Existentially, we are all alone, and each person has a unique set of keys on his / her emotional board that he / she needs to master, <u>acquiring the basic skill at the emotional level of self-growth</u> that I call **EMOTIONAL DIPLOMACY.** We need *to intellectualize our emotions and individualized the food for thought* through the <u>*Selection + Organization method*</u>, described above. <u>Every one of us has</u> a traumatized spirit due to having been exposed to life's unavoidable day-to-day fight of intelligence against ignorance or good against evil. How can one ***reach an internal equilibrium*** leaves us wondering,

Why, Why, Why? and *How, How, and How?*

The **MANUAL OF LIFE** that I call on us to work out is, in fact, the school of ***self-awareness, self-adjustment, self-installation, self-realization, and self-salvation.*** <u>These are the five basic stages of life</u> that comprise the parts of every book of mine book, meant to help us answer the questions above because each of those stages connects us to the Universal Laws of life on Earth, ***the Law of Cause and Effect*** being the core one .The **Golden Section** of inner beauty needs to be instilled as a human fractal by everyone continuously and consciously..

The Fractal of a Spiritualized Being is in the Holistic Self-Refining!

Form   +   *Content*

(Body+ Spirit+ Mind) + (Self-Consciousness + Universal Consciousness)

Having instilled in yourself the basic five steps of self-growth, you will easily work out ***your own modifications of those steps***, <u>customizing them for your own personal needs</u> because there are no two of us that think, feel, speak, and act in the same way. Your uniqueness determines your choices in life and the priorities that you single out for yourself.

The Choices We Take Dictate the Life We Live!

2. We're Unique in Every Stance; We Can Live but Only Once!

The world is full of unhappy people that seek *to satisfy their internal hunger* for the solution of their daily problems and get the answer to the question what they are here for. To answer that question, we need to take the light side of life and stay there, no matter what, adding our energy to *the Universal Energy Field* that sustains our life on Earth.

Put the Strain on Your Sub-Conscious Brain!

Such perception of life, though, demands a lot of self-education and developed consciousness, the consciousness at which we comprehend the total unity of everything, become totally aware of the immensity of life in the Universe, and actively contribute our own tiny bit to it Regrettably, rotten mentality and lack of self-consciousness are characterizing the humanity now. People read a lot of self-help books, listen to the talks of the most advanced minds, hear tons of advice from their loved ones and psychotherapists, but still do not know how to attain *the satisfaction of the internal hunger of a seeking soul.*

Establish psychic protection against any evil injection!

The problem is we need *a strategic path of action*, on the one hand, and *an individualized recipe* for each disturbed soul, on the other. However, visits to a psychologist might end up in very stereotyped recommendations, not geared to a person that seeks help. *So, don't let the weaker side of you cook a messy emotional stew! Help yourself!*

To be able to say the auto-induction below and feel quite comfortable and self-confident requires lot of work that people feel lazy about doing. Most of us spend lives bouncing back and forth between the good and evil of life. It wears out our souls and deplete us of the spirit of self-worth and a consistent life-construction.

Reflect on Your Actions and Monitor the Reactions!

3. The Quality of Life is the Newly Discovered Self-Might!

If you build yourself up holistically, *processing your grace-based wholeness in five levels*, your life will not be cast to the negative pole again and again because you'll be <u>a conscious manager of your life.</u>

(Body+ Spirit+ Mind) +

(Self-Consciousness + the Universal Consciousness)

To Unify <u>the Soul and Self-Consciousness</u> as One is

the Goal of Everyone!

----

*"The fundamental underlying cause of the difficulties and chaos conditions in the human landscape is **the lack of knowledge** and **the intolerance of people** toward their fellow humans?"(Ravi. P. S. Berg)*

So, let's try and process the self-worth though the holistically built **<u>SELF-UNIVERSE</u>** in *the physical, emotional, mental, spiritual and universal strata of life,* making " *right our might!"* !*(Richard Wetherill)*

Right is my might!

Answer the fundamental question *What am I here for?* looking deep into yourself and determining what skills, interests, hobbies, wishes, actions make you unique and *become your personal might.*

Everyone has his / her exceptional side inside, his / her unique spirit that glues *the body and mind together*. It awaits to be discovered and put forward as *the Chancellor, running your life.* So, be upbeat; follow its constructive lead! You are building your own Cathedral inside ,brick by brick!

The Strongest Energy Remains to Be the Unbeatable Spirit of Thee!

4. In My Life-Quest, I'm the Best!

Keep doing *the Auto-Suggestive Meditation* (*Stage One, 4)* every time you have a chance to relax for five minutes and feel *the necessity to boost your spirit*! In strenuous situations of life, use the main induction to calm down and regain your self-esteem. I suggest using the one below as the main back-up *(See any books on Self-Resurrection)*

I know who I am!

I am a strong, calm, bold, and determined owner of my firm will!

I can...; I want to...; and I will...!

<u>In my life's quest, I am the best!</u>

I have taught generations of my students to do different *Self-Suggestive Meditations* before each lecture and at its end, programming themselves for the goals they might be having in mind at that time. Before students leave the classroom, a different induction normally finishes the lecture, boosting their spirit and instilling self-awareness, self-control, and confidence

Be more self-aware to holistically beware!

If the students get de-focused, we perform breathing though the time and space meditation, as described above. The students always welcome such play-time interval, and they feel refreshed and inspired after it. They report to me continuously, how *much stronger in spirit they become*, and how much more determined to accomplish what they are dreaming of they are.

I do my self-inducting consistently, too, breathing in one part of the induction, breathing out the other one. The possibilities are endless. You can always make up your own inspirational inductions. One requirement, though - *the inductions should rhyme in the mind's twine!* Again, according to Edgar Cayce,

"The Rhyming Word goes Better Inward."

5. Stabilize Your Emotional Surf!

Calm Yourself!

No doubt, the emotional stabilization is the most challenging task in building the self-worth on the emotional plane of life. Our lives are overwhelmed with all kinds of problems and tribulations, and life often gets bad before it gets better. In any disbalancing situation, process the problem through the same **HOLISITIC GRID** of the *physical, emotional, mental, spiritual,* and *universal stabilization,* inducting the mind-set "**So-o-o** *(breathing in)* **- Ha-a-a-m**"*(breathing out)* repeatedly.

Life is going on (in) *, and it's beautiful in my own form!* (out)

Check out the *state of your health,* calm your *emotional pendulum,* see what *mental information* is needed to put your mind in charge, verify the *authenticity of your actions* spiritually, and ,finally, ascertain *the path you are on your life goal-wise.* Such **SELF-SCANNING** in five levels should become *a set of positive skills* to develop.

Don't get de-magnetized by a self-waste bite!

Science proves that 98% of people waste their unique potential in the negative - positive vibrations stream. On the *- / 0 / + axis* of life vibrations, we need to stay *in the zero position of inner balance* and equanimity. It is the solar plexus spot on the palm. If you put the three central fingers together, you'll get the cross that we protect ourselves with in time and space.

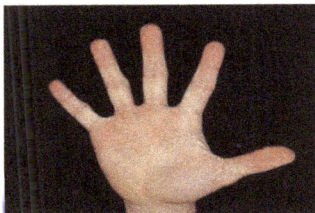

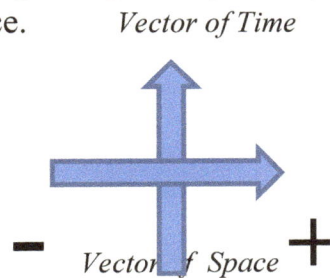

Vector of Time

$-$ *Vector of Space* $+$

Centralize your emotions, inducting a famous mind-set by *King Solomon* that was engraved on his ring and that he used as a reminder of the relativity of life. It will help you *stabilize your negative–positive pendulum* that any life situation puts in motion. Life is going on, and it's beautiful in any form!

"It Too Shall Pass!"

6. To Build an Emotional Fort, Master Your Love World!

Next, and most importantly, *our emotional lives are governed by the love ties!* The love job has many responsibilities, the most challenging of which is *being noble inside.* The inner and outer beauty is always based on a person's nobility that in turn, is always linked to the ability for **SELF-TAMING**. True love is the search of *a partner in spirituality,* not just in physical expression.

Love-Gaining is in Self-Taming!

In my last book *"The State of Love from the Above"* and its second edition *"Love Ecology,"* I address the necessity to scan the authenticity of your love relationship in the *physical, emotional, mental, spiritual,* and *universal dimensions* before legalizing your love with marriage. In other words, I suggest *studying love as a multi-dimensional entity.* Like everything else in life, love is a process that needs to be monitored consciously, delicately, and respectfully. *(See the book" Self-Taming')*

Regrettably, *respect is lost from the concept of love* that therefore, lost its sacredness nowadays, being replaced with *shamelessness and the display of inner ugliness*! Not to come to the point of no return, make a life's U-turn! Self-programming must be inspirational and refining!

It takes only a stroke to change the minus into a plus!

Overwhelmed with ignorance and living on the automatic drive, people are wasting their love ability, depleting themselves of *love energy that is not re-fillable.* The love-rehearsing games that suck you in end up in your inner emptiness and lower your self-worth to the point that only arrogance and anger remain. Only by the end of life do we realize that nothing really matters, in the long run, more than the people we love and those that love us in return. So, keep inducting yourself with,

Demagnetization of Love Kills the Self-Worth Stuff!

Be the Chosen One to Save the World from the Simulated Love!

(The sculpture by Etienne Pirot)

Love is Blessed from the Above;
Hallelujah to the Eternal Love!

7. Self-Worth is Our Love's Boss!

Next, staying on the path of accumulating self-worth and raising self-consciousness, we develop *the ability to love and deserve the love in return in time and space, not in a one-night race.*

"Dance Me to the End of Love!"

(Leonard Cohen - a Canadian poet and a musician)

Your self-worth is tested by your ability to love, to commit, to be responsible for the life that is entrusted to you, and never be negligent of the life that you bring into this world

.*At present, our ability to love is tested by our attitude to money.* *Carl Yung* is teaching us to see through a person in this respect, saying

"If a person is cheap with money, he'll be cheap in love."

Love in its holistic value is neglected now . We have brought love to a shameless level of *"Sex sells!"* that brings the sanctity of true love to an anachronism, ruled by an immediate gratification whim, on the one hand, and the society's lack of morals on the other.

Love, however, is not just an emotional stuff. It is directly connected to our intelligence. Therefore, it's very important to enrich intelligence and raise the self-consciousness in the relationship, not to come down to the status of a limited "*home cow."(Somerset Maugham).*

This is how a great British writer very objectively characterizes the attitude of different sexes to love. *"Women can think and talk about love all day long; men only at times."*

Only a common goal in self-realization that considers the self-growth plans of both parties can keep us together for years on end, *making love our Perpetua mobile*. So, solarize your soul with consideration, intelligence, confidence, kindness, and self-control! Be the self-worth model! Generate the feeling of the inner might over your weak side.

Break Your Bad Habits Spell; Better Yourself!

8. Holistic Self-Worth Accumulation is Based on Love Elation!

The new times are the times of <u>our transcendence into a new mode of life</u> - *new thinking, speaking, feeling ,and acting*, generated by the technological evolution and the exponential growth of the means of seeing life through a celestially digitized perception of a new spiritual reality that is also an emerging **NEW LOVE REALITY**.

The power of God is in everyone's digitized thought!

The ever-quoted religious and spiritual maxima *"God is Love!"* and *"Marriages are made in Heaven!"* are commonly repeated, but we are still in search of <u>the godly love</u> in a man / woman while the spiritual deterioration of the best of God's creation is appalling now.

The skill to love in mass must be instilled and developed in us!

So, the first thing that we need to look for in a person is a **GODLY SPARK OF LOVE** in his / her heart and the drops of kindness in the actions, not his / her sexual orientation. The spark of love needs to be fueled in every one of us, *becoming the torch of love,* like Danco's heart. According to the ancient legend, Danco tore his heart out of his chest to lighten up the way for the people, walking in darkness.

Love in sync with the soul; be spiritually whole!

Luckily and irreversibly, a present-day man has started perceiving himself <u>as an integral part of the whole of life</u>, *not as a separate, fearful, society indoctrinated, and dependable personage* who plays his part in the performance of life in which every role is scripted.

The most advanced, well-read, and forward-thinking people *activate their new genetic code* and stand up for the uniqueness of their transforming Self. They are swimming against the current of the generally accepted trend of *a savagely expressed love.*

"As it is Above", so it is Below!"

9. Love-Gaining is in Self-Taming!

The work at love is a hard stuff! The Indian mystic and a very wise man, Sadhguru, recommends we restrain our urge for sex relationships when we are too young and are not yet accomplished in any way. *"Don't rush to love too early!"* Love is a skill that must be studied.

LOVE EDUCATION is urgently needed to redirect the minds of the young to the sacredness of love and the importance of retaining it for life. The sense of mutual responsibility in love must be planted as a seed for pure love feeling to proceed. Again,

Love is an Art! Be smart!

Meanwhile, overwhelmed with ignorance and living on the automatic drive*, we are wasting our love ability, depleting ourselves of love energy that is not re-fillable*. Love-rehearsing games suck us in and enlarge inner emptiness that lowers self-worth to the point that only arrogance and anger remain. The shift of the priorities from self-growth to self-pleasuring inevitably ruins a person's ability to create himself. Love gets in the way and demands making the choice,

The choices we make dictate the life we live!

The present-day reality pushes us to making the choice in favor of our *Self-Installation* professionally and *Self-Realization* personally. It's only natural, but it doesn't mean that we need to exclude love from self-creation. Love makes us much better and more inspired, and it needs to be incorporated into our intellectually spiritualized self-growth.

Science has it that *we tend to couple with someone of opposite brain dominance,* so that left-brained types supplement the mates with right dominance. The possibility of marrying your missing inner half has great implications in the reason why right-married men are more successful in life than single ones.

So, Is Marriage a Bliss or a Curse?

That's also the Problem of Self-Worth!

10. Love Domain is in Every One's Vein!

Right marrying , though, is not a gift from the Above; it's the ability that needs to ripen. In my last book *"Love Ecology,"* I recommend scanning your partner for the compatibility in the *physical, emotional, mental, spiritual, and universal* dimensions, starting preferably form the Above – the discussion of the universal dreams of your partner and his / her aspirations in <u>realizing the God-granted exceptionality</u>.

<u>What signature of self-worth will you leave on Earth?</u>

Be sure to probe the religious, *spiritual values, mental richness, emotional sanity, and finally, the physical fitness* of the feelings that will be much more blossoming with true, faithful, and committed love. Don't just look for the same qualities in your partner and do not try to change him / her verbally or with numerous demands and empty expectations

Sameness is boring; differences don't bite; they unite!

Science proves that <u>people get rotten inside with sexual misconduct and an" ass-cult" all over the world</u>. Hopefully, the impact of the scientific progress in the field of rejuvenation, backed up with the exponential growth of technology will pave the way where the impulsivity to catch the fading glimpse of sexual energy will not push people to cheating, making someone's self-worth consideration a cognitive reality.

The point is, we are living at the time of new perception of the reality in which *life is the digital text, and we are its programmers and its editors.* <u>The magnetic field around the heart is 20% stronger that of the mind, and</u> when we have the **HEART+ MIND** sync in action in our relationships, at work, in the realization of our unique goals, **we magnetize our core, our self-worth and develop the multi-dimensional field** around us that <u>gets integrally connected</u> to the informational magnetic field of the Earth and the universe.

So, Make the Heart Smart and the Mind Kind! Be One of a Kind!

11. Don't Love Negligently, Love Intelligently!

You're Who you Love and How! Wow!

Don't see Sex Liberation as your Ultimate Destination!
Avoid a cheap sex trap. Be in a strong mental wrap!

Be Charming and Sex-Appealing. Be Soul-Refining,
but not Love-Whining!

Men hope that women they marry will never change,
but they do!
Women hope that men they marry will change,
but they don't!

" In a relationship's fate, you are the master of the word that's Not said! But you're the slave of the one that flew ahead." (Aram Hayami)

So, tame your tongue for the love fun!

Never Stop to Implement Your Love Enrichment!

The Kaleidoscope of Your Soul Must Shine with Self-Control!

12. Marriage is a Test for the Self-Worth Wealth!

Marriage is the most vital decision that literally changes the life of those that make it. It requires a lot of **personal integrity** that needs to be developed in a person before he makes that decision. Both parties, they must consciously commit to taking it seriously for years to come.

Unfortunately, in many cases, marriage, especially for women, seems to be the dream that that they have been nurturing for years , and when the opportunity arises, the imaginary fun and the aura of an exaggerated self-worth is blurring the reality.

*"**Moral relativism**"(Sigmund Fraud) **is ruining our love optimism**!*

For starters, marriage is a multi-dimensional entity, too It needs **physical, emotional, mental, spiritual, and universal scanning** on the on-going basis. Life together for months or years helps to scan the self-worth of a person of your choice, but it must be kept in mind that every action we take in life either magnifies its inner core, or a person's self-worth, or it de-magnetizes it in the course of life together.

Love Psychology is based on Self-Ecology!

We cannot save a marriage just relying on the psychologist who can hardly help you in a few sessions, unless you yourself do deep **analysis of your self-worth and your partner's matching it or surpassing it**.

It is impossible, though, to qualify a person's self-worth correctly if he / she is heart-broken, mentally unstable, linguistically negligent, and self-knowledge ignorant. Integrity means the unity of physical. emotional, mental., spiritual, and universal realms of a person's **HEART + MIND** link, reflected best in the co-dependent life. Love is the reflection of the mind+ heart connection. connection!

It's Easy to Say," I Want You."

It's Much Harder to Utter, " I Need You!"

13. Love Consciousness is a Mess!

Our present-day *love consciousness is a mess!* It's the time of *sex* liberation and sex emancipation. Unfortunately, this process of a free will expression has gone far beyond the boundaries of decency and shamefulness. The virus of cheating and casual sex destroys the concept of matrimony in its core.

Be able to bounce back in the spirit of love in fact!

Seeing a psychotherapist can hardly help when the souls are infected with corruption , fear and love distruction.. Like the corona virus , we need social distancing and the quarantine for those that destroy the hearts and minds of the young. It's extremely hard to outshine those that are vile. . That's why, love education is supposed to turn the minds from love frustration to love elation!

You cannot coach Love; it's a rich soul's stuff!

Personal freedom is exaggerated now, marriages have turned into expensive shows, the authenticity of love feelings has become a point of mistrust, lying, and fun-mining. That is not to say, though, that true love has left our hearts' premises. Sincere love is still the life stuff!

"I understand your heart; you understand mine. That's our love twine!"

Next, the search for soul mates has become digital, but the attitude to love has become more deceptive and very superficial. The sense of glamor that many shallow shows and programs promote instills a wrong idea in our minds to treat love as a game and keep flipping the coin, instead of raising our *love consciousness.*

Among other things, love is not just granted from the Above, it's earned by a person who is able to magnetize it with his moral, committed, goal-oriented, and *spiritually intelligent* SELF-GRAVITY, *not self-vanity.*

Love Relationship and a Matrimony are the Means for Joint Self-Growth.

For Love to Work, Do the Talk!

Consensus in Love is a Pure Stuff!

14. Your Personal Psychology is in Love Ecology.

Life has proven that behind every successful man is an intelligent, love-motivated woman. Matrimony becomes not just a monetarily sealed bond, it's the way **to self-realize the individual dreams and fulfill the lives together.**" I suggest getting more serious and holistically oriented in making the choice of a partner not for a one-night stand, a month, or some years, but for life, processing your feelings through **the multi-dimensional grid** - _physical, emotional, mental, spiritual, and universal_. You will better complement each other on the path of Self-Realization in life.

X-ray the partner of our choice in five dimensions of his / her love's voice.

Indeed, previous generations fell in love and got married at a much younger age. They also stayed together longer because they were not so self-installation oriented. The financial status of a man helped a woman make her choice and feel protected. **Our personal growth has come to the forefront of love at the end of the last century, and it's an evolutionary demand now.** The necessities of cooking, and self-grooming are less burdensome , but the pressure of competition and the new technological times demand a rigorous self-installation professionally and more personal improvement spiritually. .Love is growing by **the same stages of self-growth:**

Self-Awareness _(physical level)_ ; Self- Monitoring _(emotional level)_; Self-Installation _(mental level)_; Self-Realization _(spiritual level)_, and Self-Salvation _(universal level)_

It is truly intriguing to be more intelligent and much less compulsive in constructing the love life that is governed by the holistic rules of the left-right brains connection, strategic selection of a love partner, and conscious love formation. **Love ecology is becoming our psychology!**

There's No Love Elation without Self-Growth Stabilization!

15. Marriage Gravity is Not Built on Self-Vanity!

Love can't be blind any more. *Self-vanity must be substituted by self-worth in love seeking and lovemaking!* Marriage now should be based on true, holistically formed love that embraces all <u>five levels of self-development</u> - *universal aspirations* (the life-monitoring dream beyond materialistic and egotistic standpoints, *the spiritual growth* in life, *mental baggage* and mutual understanding, *emotional conformity* and finally, *the physical matching* – all stages as an aware recognition of the vibratory clicking in the *physical + emotional + mental+ spiritual+ universal realms of life*, governed by the holistic paradigm:

Self-Synthesis ⟹ **Self-Analysis** ⟹ **Self-Synthesis**!

⬇ ⬇ ⬇

(self-awareness) ➡ *(self-monitoring +self-installation +self-realization)* ➡ *(self-salvation)*

Marriage is the holistic ability of both partners to share their space and time on the mutual spine of love!

Only then will the viruses of casual sex, quick fix relationships, and constant cheating that have put our humanity at the brink of **MORAL DEMAGNITIZATION** be reversed. Then, we'll be able to re-program our minds to *the three fundamentals life* by *Ravi Berg.*

"REJECT + RESIST + REFORM"

or not to be love- upset, control your

BODY + MIND + SEX set!

Interestingly, *Sigmund Freud* considered falling in love to be a complex mental process," *a sort of hypnosis* "which is in accord with the present-day *neurologic understanding of love* that claims that love has the mental basis and is located not in the heart, but in the mind.

Love is Mutual Magnetization, based on Conscious Life Elation!

16. Love Infinity Develops Character Ability!

A person's self-worth is being formed in the process of character formation that should never end. The earlier we start paying attention to shaping our kids' character, their idea of true love and the good and bad in life , their ability to say " No!" to things that are unacceptable in a family life and the social environment, the stronger and more magnetized the process of <u>the core formation of character</u> will be in a child.

A great Russian poet *Vladimir Mayakovski* in his instructive poem of what is good and bad for kids gives us the main, easily digestible standpoint that needs to be prioritized. ***"The orchards will bloom in a blast if you learn to tell yourself,*** <u>*" I Can!" and I Must!"*</u>

This mind-set must be instilled in the subconscious mind of kids with the basic values and virtues that need to be developed throughout life. The essential one is , of course, the **ABILITY TO LOVE** and be loved in return that must be developed with grace that is innate in us.

Love education without frustration must be mastered with grace and inner elation!

A well-known digital biologist and a medical philosopher *Dr. Bruce Lipton* says that we can reform the matrix of the subconscious mind that determines the habitual patterns of behavior ***only through love***, or as *Dr Lipton* suggests by *"taking the red pill."*

Literally, when we are in love, we get inspired ***to be exceptional and truly authentic.*** The mind that is subconsciously ruling 95 % of our lives stays in the background voiceless. ***Love becomes our conscious boss!*** Conscious loving guarantees love sanity, commitment, compassion, and consideration in a relationship. Obviously, s***elf-worth is growing with the authentic love force!***

Love Sanity is built on Love Gravity!

17. Love Gravity is formed by the Fractals of Self-Symmetry!

Accumulating self-worth, develop also the habit of *flooding your body with higher consciousness in the morning and before going to bed.*

Help your love be consciously fed, and never stop making yourself better! Be a self-guru! *"Be like Me; I am the Way!"* (*Jesus Christ*) In fact, spiritual maturity helps develop self-symmetry in us

Self-Symmetry is in a Self-Sustained Love - Gravity!

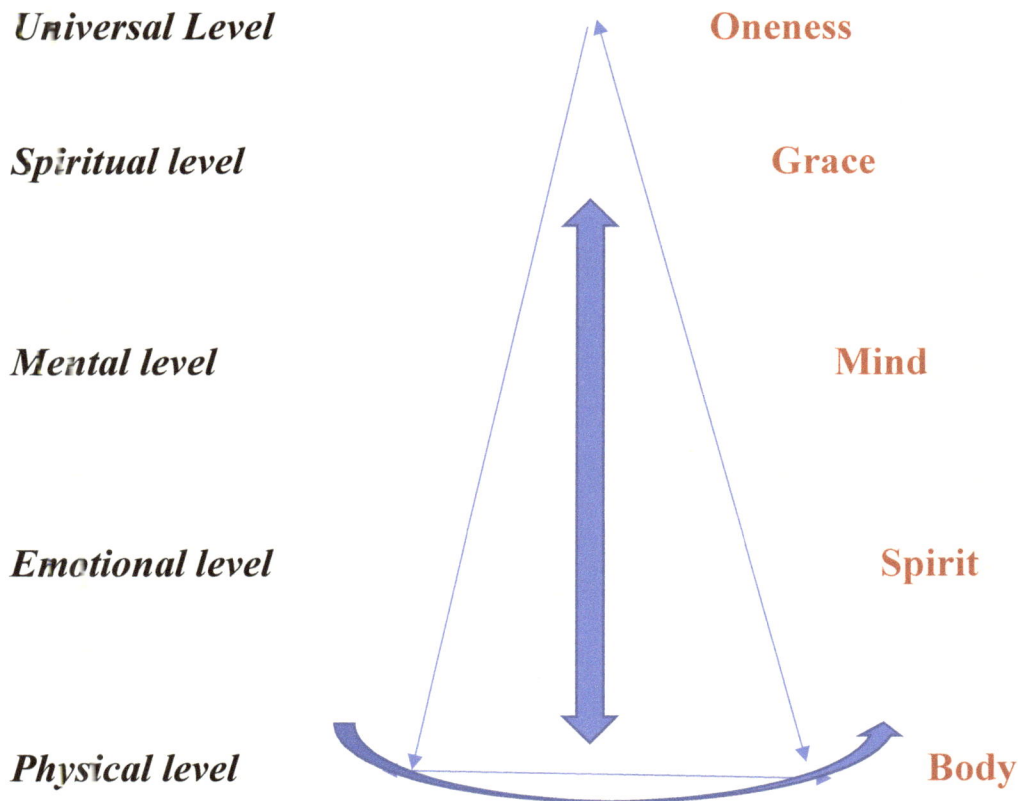

Universal Level	Oneness
Spiritual level	Grace
Mental level	Mind
Emotional level	Spirit
Physical level	Body

BODY + SPIRIT + MIND + GRACE + ONENESS = A WHOLE YOU!

X-ray your feelings though these five levels for *the gravity of love and the self-worth magnetic force.* Scan your *body* for its health, the *spirit* for its positive charge, the *mind* for its awareness, *inner* **grace** for its kindness, and the feeling of *Oneness* for the beauty of life .

Live and Love by the Eternal Symmetry of Love!

18. Expand the Inner Circle of Resistance to the Poison of Life!

Never stop strengthening your *intellectual culture linguistically, emotionally, professionally, culturally, and socially.* Self- creation is an integral process that goes holistically in every level. The necessity to train ourselves to respond to life mentally as opposed to reacting emotionally gets fixed into our *virtual matrix* now only if we are aware of the importance of shaping our minds. Your auto-induction must be:

I must be mindful and bold to fit into a new life's mold!

We all make mistakes and have sins of wrong thinking, saying, and doing. Specifically, we need to realize what we had done wrong not to get into the vortex of more wrongdoing by force of habit.

The inner matrix should be personalized, not digitized or robotized!

It appears that only with the belief in God and real rationalization of thinking; governed by the emotional intelligence, can we resist, reject, and reform our imperfect inner uniform. The words of a great British writer *Somerset Maugham* are very convincing here ,

"The mills of God grind slowly, but they grind exceed small!"

There is another point to consider. We cannot be weak for a long time. The people that get discouraged or depressed, those that resort to drugs or alcohol and justify themselves with being too stressed out, *sink into the psycho-holes* that they are unable to get from because they do not blame themselves for the weaknesses that demagnetize their personal core.

"General demagnetization of a spirit always starts and finishes with the brain!"(Dr. Fred .Bell) Therefore, it is vital to incentivize yourself and others with love for life, compassion, understanding, mercy, self-belief, and or self- actualization in life. Don't let yourself fall into the depression stall. Therefore, I totally agree with *Antony Robins* here,

"Depression is a Self-Inflicted Disease!"

19. To Be a Self-Programmed Love Cell - Tame Yourself!

Rabbi P. S. Berg, that I have quoted above, writes that we should tame *the three beasts* that get us into the disbalance of *(Sex + Body+ Mind)* because we prioritize sex over the mind. Rabbi Berg's calls on us to establish order in life and reverse the life from the disbalance of **666** *(the symbol of death)* to **999** *(the symbol of life)*, putting sex. under the control of the mind. *(Mind + Body + Sex)*

We need to tame the body like we tame an animal!

Love is the emotion of intelligence because intelligence is life itself! You can change your brain only in unity with the heart. So ,*you need to re-condition the body for a new mind*, and do it in the auto-suggestive, or self-hypnotizing way. *We should change the brain only in unity with the heart.* *(See the book " Soil-Refining!")* It's like planting the seeds of love into the barren, rocky soil. The soils need a lot of nurturing with love intelligence.

Unfortunately, there is a tendency now *to redirect the Universal Love Flow and let the mind respond to the body*. Such situation generates a completely distorted perception of life and its generator – love. The hormones display should not be more meaningful and valuable than intelligence! I think that a distorted love-emancipated position of a woman is responsible for the appearance of many deviations from the regular *"stream of consciousness technique."* (James Joyce)

Women need to reflect on their being the embodiment of beauty, balance, and love and focus on their femininity and fragility, not letting men forget the role of their loving mothers in their maturation. A woman's role of a mother, a lover, a friend, a stabilizer of a family, and *the center of its Solar System* needs to be restored and respected.

Better Your Love Stride in Five Dimensions of life!

20. Forgiveness doesn't Change the Past, but It does Change the Future!

According to *Dr. Joe Dispenza* and his wonderful book "**Becoming Supernatural**," we are quite literary supernatural by nature if given the proper knowledge and instructions, if we stop being race nationality and religious affiliations prejudiced. He writes, *" Don't brainwash yourself! Beat the bad habits that you keep repeating every day. Become supernatural, per say!"*

Only he who keep his head will go ahead!

It's known that a person who had committed something bad suffers from the remorse and the ruined self-worth. He feels sorry for himself, tries hard to justify his action and has grudges against someone, and living in the past. So, forgive yourself and clean up your guilty cell! Living in the past programs your mind for another mistake.

"The familiar past becomes a predictable future."

"Problems are the circuits of circumstances in the brain"(Dr. Dispenza) If we re-wire our brains intentionally, problems become the steppingstones in a new relationship because the negative experience **gets processed consciously through the grid of five-dimensional wisdom** (physical, emotional, mental spiritual, and universal).

If you analyze why you have failed in each of these areas consciously, you will reason out that it was the period of your self-growth that is very beneficial for your love relationship or your social outreach. If we are **objective in our self-judgement**, life stops being the routine, and you get out of the crisis with more self-worth and confidence" Viewed from this perspective, *forgiveness means establishing order back in life* and obtaining the self-worth ground - the basis for a new life program, incentivized with new love.

Don't Be the Victim of Your Twisted Self; Reform Yourself!

Karma is Our Eternal Drama!

(Alyx Dellamonica - Creation of the Korean Sculptor Do Kho-So)

Why Don't We Try and Turn Our Karma
into Its Darma?

21. To Change Your Karma Role, Take Care of Your Soul!

Holistically re-programming bad habits into good skills, we are lifting the karma of our wrong-doings and developing the **INTUITION** that is our indicator of what needs to be de-programmed and re-programmed. Intuition is also is our direct line to God.

Life-gaining is in self-taming!

It is literary so because self-taming strengthens health and the immune system of a willful person. *Dr Boris Uvaidov* writes, *"The inner environment of a person, the energy of his chakras, his thoughts, words, and feelings affect the content of his / her blood!"* So, good, clean blood constitutes the inner environment that kills the poisonous bacteria in the gut - our second brain. Taming impulsivity, irritability and anger ,we save the blood from being polluted with the negative particles that accumulate in the blood. The law of attraction works in both directions in this respect. Your negativity attracts more ruinous events and negative people into your life. Paradoxically, people go to church, pray, meditate, light up candles, but they hardly practice what they preach in action.

Fix the Antenna in your brain. Tame yourself in God's domain!

Naturally, we need to be very picky with the people that we allow into our lives. So, get rid of all the complaining, needy, and judgmental people. Cut them from your on-line and phone communication. I, for one, stopped being open with women for years, not to be contaminated by materialistic limitedness, heartless egoism, ignorance, loveless demands, and complains about their men. Sincerity has become a communication rarity!

Self-worth gaining is in self- worth sustaining!

Life is not a Rehearsal; It's Your Refection in it as a Person!

22. Emotional Gravity is Charged by Wisdom, Not Love Treason!

Concluding the emotional level of self-worth formation, we need to remember that our values and virtues are getting shaped from the earliest age, and both our parents and grandparents *contribute a lot to our inner world* that later becomes our own responsibility.

"Wisdom is supreme; therefore, get wisdom."(*Proverbs 4 :7*)

I remember my grandfather come up to my bed when I was half asleep with the Bible and read some verses from it over me, praying in the old Slavic language, not understandable to me. I was only five years old then, but the image of him, standing on his knees near my bed makes me chill with the sacredness of his love and faith, his sincere wish to protect me from any evil. It was in the socialist state where only old people went to church, having been raised in the pre-revolutionary Russia. My grandmother wouldn't let me go to bed if I had a fight with my brother. She would wake me up to make peace with him, saying,

"Remember, evil must not out-grow the love flow!"

I did not understand much of that saying then, but her insistence that I pray to *"Our Father"* in the morning for a good day and say thanks to *the Sun, the Moon, the Angels, and all the living beings on Earth* became the ritual of my life and helped me accumulate the emotional gravity and diplomacy ever since. When I tried to re-educate her, saying, *"Granny, we're taught - there's no God,"* she would patiently reassure me with the words that got engraved in my heart and mind,

"Socialism is not for ever; God is forever! Learn to be grateful to Him and avoid the sin!"

In sum, the spiritual basis for self-worth is planted in our souls during the entire life. It gets solidified by our sense of gratitude and wisdom.

Breathe in Gratitude and Breathe out Attitude!

Stage Three

(The Mental Level of Self-Scanning)

Self-Worth
Enrichment

*We're climbing **the Tree of Self-Knowledge** to destroy the storage of the imperfect human understanding of **the Tree of Life!***

Upload your smart phone with a New Mental Tone!
*(Sort out the inspirational mind-sets in the file **Self-Resurrection** in five levels-physical, emotional, mental, spiritual, universal. Have them at hand as the **Self-Help Hypnotherapy**)*

Self-Worth is Rising on the Intellectual Horizon!

Our Spiritual Maturation is in Learning Without Frustration!

(Etienne Pirot)

Knowledge is the Bliss! The More we Know; the Lighter the Life Burden is!

1. "Mind over Matter" is Our Self-Worth Strata!

To begin the mental level of self-worth forming, I'm calling on you here to develop your intelligence beyond any limits and irrespective of any life tribulations. *(See the Global Award Winner book "Living Intelligence or the Art of Becoming! "/ 2020)*

To develop beyond the earthly limitations of cosmic and **SELF GRAVITY**, we should stop arguing about religion and spirituality vs. science that are just the sides of the same coin and *start looking at life as a digital phenomenon* in which we are parts of the universal system. *Digital intelligence* is enveloping us everywhere, and it is governing us though self-evolution as particles in the universal entirety, without considering our race, country, age, religious affiliation, or a monetary status. So, let's unite every conceptual difference of our definition of *"God"* under one common thought - *Spirituality, the Universal Intelligence,* or *the Master Mind*. It's everywhere, no doubt about it!

The present-day development of a person's general and emotional intelligence means that it is enriched by the artificial intelligence, leading the humanity to a new stage of consciousness - *Super-Consciousness.* Your self-assessment and constant self-reflection will prompt to you the plan of action to accomplish the holistic unity of self-worth in a fractal formation of an intelligently spiritualized being.

Body + Spirit + Mind + Self-Consciousness + Universal Consciousness!

The uniqueness of everyone's soul and its earthly self-expression should be in the soul's holistic unity that helps one fulfill his / her divine plan of action that is, in fact, each other's life mission. No one can do it better for you than yourself! Obviously, it is the mind that we must start working on, following the main scientific strata –" *Mind over Matter!"*

Be Wise! Optimize - Strategize - Actualize!

2. Vistas of Intelligence to Mount

Any self-growth is backed up by **the growth of intelligence** that is shaping a personality level by level holistically in the form *the Russian dolls, incorporated inside by the Mother Doll.* The holistic knowledge of **ten vistas of intelligence** (*See the chart below*) will shape your general outlook that is vital for Self-Realization of your unique potential at the amazing time of our technological expansion.

10. Universal Intelligence	**Super-Level of Consciousness**
9. Spiritual Intelligence	Universal — **Self-Salvation**
8. Social Intelligence	**Macro- Level**
7. Cultural Intelligence	Spiritual -**Self-Realization**
6. Financial Intelligence	**Mezzo- Level**
5. Professional Intelligence	Mental - **Self-Installation**
(Creative Intelligence)	
4. Psychological Intelligence	**Meta- Level**
3 Emotional Intelligence	**Emotional— Self-Monitoring**
`2. Language Intelligence	**Mini-Level**
1. General Intelligence	Physical - **Self-Awareness**
(Cognitive / Digital)	

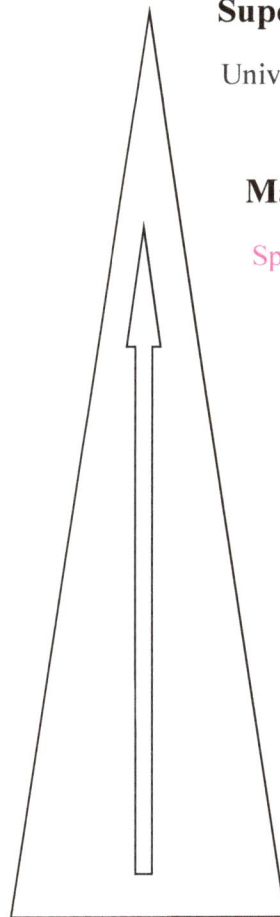

"Disconnection of knowledge is the death of self-power."

(*Schopenhauer*)

Self-creation is impossible without constant self-improvement.

Don't Self-Strife, Let Mind Rule Your Life!

3. Intelligence and Self-Worth Must Be in Force!

Our new, exponentially developing technological world needs a lot of intelligence to be applied to any expertise as per the demands of the reality that we are trying to digitally manage in time and space. .

"Knowledge is the origin of the sense of Self!"(Carl Yung)

AWARE ATTENTION paid to the avalanche of information that we must process consciously is badly needed now. Developing aware attention requires *a special skill* that will allow a professional *to sort out the valid information* from the rest of its heterogeneous bulk and get it stored in the brain's memory to be used timely and effectively, following the paradigm: .

Generalize – Internalize - Personalize – Strategize - Actualize!

Synthesis – Analysis -Synthesis!

In my five books on *Self-Resurrection*, I keep reminding you of the necessity to process knowledge through *the grid of five dimensions (physical, emotional, mental spiritual, and universal)* to form <u>an indispensable core of a personality,</u> its **SELF-GRAVITY!** Like the Earth has its gravity, we, as its indispensable parts have it, too, and the richer the self-worth of a person, the stronger his / her self-gravity, or his / her *exceptionality* is.

The process of the professional *Self-Installation* that the mental level presupposes demands a person's dedication in his *exceptionality* that is always built on the sense of self-worth , or *charisma*, accumulated by a person over the years of the dedication <u>to the dream that exposes this exceptionality</u> if a person pursues it with self-confidence and faith.

Such people mesmerize us, and we gravitate to their personalities not because they are worth millions or even billions of dollars , but because their sense of self-worth creates an aura of personal magnetism, self-discipline, self-control, and amazing intelligence that in sync reward them with success.

Self-Worth is a Self-Gravity Force!

4. Self-Installation is the Process of Self-Worth Formation!

Professional intelligence is central in your growth on the ladder of life-forming intelligences (*See "Living Intelligence or the Art of Becoming*!). In fact, a person's self-realization is based on ***the enrichment of professional intelligence*** that is nurturing his / her self-worth,

Living is learning , and learning is living!

We need to always remember that academic learning and getting professional intelligence is just <u>the starting part of your life.</u> Your professional and personal growth need to be continued throughout life in an ascending fashion of constant bettering yourself in five dimensions - *physically, emotionally, mentally, spiritually, and universally.* If you stop learning, your conscious perception of the reality will get stuck and the process of inner degradation and stagnation will begin.

The one who stops learning is literally dying!

With the exponential growth of technology, the knowledge that we have today gets outdated tomorrow. So, going to bed every day, on top of ***scanning your day in five dimensions,*** ask yourself the undeniably vital question:

<u>What have I learnt today?</u>

Ask yourself how you have improved in every dimension and what you have reasoned out better in life. Knowledge is boundless! It must be accumulated holistically in every level and ***processed consciously.*** The most motivational words by *Socrates* are to be remembered here.

"I know that I know nothing; the rest don't know even that!"

Every stage of intelligence on the Pyramid of learning must be enriched constantly not to stagnate professionally and personally.

Only Knowledge Put to Action is Power!

5. Knowledge Provides Mental Fruition and Boosts Intuition!

The magnetic power of a person's self-worth is always his intelligence, wisdom, and the ability to share them with others. We gravitate to those who have **developed professional intelligence and see the reality in its full bloom,** in its both negative and positive vibrations, as opposed to those people who are led astray by immediate gratification seeking and making impulsive decisions. *As King Solomon's wisdom states,*

> *" He will die for the lack of discipline, led astray by his own great folly."(Proverbs 5:23).*

People of an exceptional self-worth and personal magnetism try to always stay **_in the zero position of the time-space vector of life._** *(Stage Two, 1)* They never swing too much to the negative pole or get carried away by the positive one. They have, what I call, **SELF-SANITY** that is the core of self-confidence and is essential in forming the *self-worth gravity*. Our inner gravity is in link with *the gravity of the Earth,* and it is connected to the Universal Intelligence through our personal antennas of **AWARE ATTENTION.** The intuitive insights gravitate to the magnetic core of a strong, disciplined, goal-focused mind.

Intuition is also fed by sifted intelligence and personal wisdom, fortified by discipline and magnetically strong self-worth. Like King Solomon, who had the ring with the words , engraved on it " **It too shall Pass,"** you must stay resilient to failures and tribulations, remembering that they will pass, too, helping the spirit actualize your dream.

The people of self-worth never demagnetize their personal gravity.

Their mind-boggling ideas are developed by the **selection and self-organization** *(See Stage One,8)* of their goal-oriented, *left + right brain* linked intelligence. The whole brain formation is their elation!

Not to get off the Personal Sanity Track, keep Your Brain Intact!

6. A Man is the Product of His Own Thoughts and Words!

The famous words by Mahatma Gandhi, " *A man is the product of his own thoughts. What he is thinking, he is becoming!"* are proven by the neuro-science and have been verified by the lives of the best people on Earth.

Brain over matter is our common strata!

Brain + Thought = Matter + Idea The evolutionary road of the humanity is on the path of an exponential development of intelligence and self-consciousness. The materialization of our thinking has become the reality for those who accept it and follow the cosmic laws, with the *Law of Attraction* in the lead . The character of man is formed by the age of thirty-five, an approximate age of Jesus Christ, and it is an irreversible truth that unless a person changes his *thinking, speaking, feeling, and acting*, no one will be ever do it for him.

The mind-set I can…! I want to…! And I will…! *strengthens the willpower steal!*

To break the negative patterns of thinking, repeat this mind-set continuously, finishing each one of them the way you need it. Thus, *you will create firm synoptic links* , forming the neurological circuits.

I'm nervous . ⟹ I'm calm and stable!

I'm very sick. ⟹ I'm strong and healthy!

I' m not lovable. ⟹ I love and I'm loved in return! etc.

Self -love, based on consciously perceived and developed self-worth as the **GRAVITATIONAL FORCE** of a human being determines our actions and protects us from compulsiveness and unconscious reactions. Self-love is ruling our outer world. Have it aboard!!

Love Physiology + Love Psychology = A Healthy Mind's Ecology!

7. Don't Get Insane; Befriend Your Brain!

Our life is getting more and more complicated and overloaded with information that speeds up the tempo of our life and makes it more automatic. No wonder the words " *It's crazy!*" are used too often now to characterize life and the uncontrollable events that occur in it

. *So, becoming calmer, smarter, and more logical is the demand of our time and the self-sanity twine.*

No doubt, you have heard about the necessity to train your brain. A lot of different electronic games, books, and all kinds of advice can be found on the Internet. I want to just remind you of **the simplest methods** to boost your memory, the critical thinking skills, and the sense of self-worth essential in the present-day informational turmoil.

1. __Don't burry your brain in the everyday routine.__ Your brain works on the neural connections and when you change those connections and do some routine things differently, your exercise your brain and make it more agile. You may change the roads you drive by, or go for a walk, cook different food, visit other cafes, go to the places that you visit rarely, like museums and theatres, or listen to the classic music, even though jazz can appeal to you most.

Variety is the spice of life!

2. __Reading has become an anachronism__ for those who cherish their egoism! "*I work. I have no time*" is a regular excuse of some of my students who prefer to plagiarize the ideas of others, not to overload their brains. They hardly ever read, if at all.

We don't live at the time of reading romantic novels or keeping diaries. That was people's occupation of the previous centuries. We live at the age of the exponential growth of information that we need to sift and up-load into our brains consciously. We need to select information for our **physical, emotional, mental, spiritual, and universal enrichment.** Elon Musk, for example, when asked what his favorite books were, named the best books of the most famous science fiction masters, books on mystery, fantasy, and mathematics. That's what I mean when I write about the necessity to build up your self-growth, **developing aware attention** to the information you process, the people that you socialize with, and the food you eat. Be life-upbeat!

:Selection + Self-Organization = Self-Construction

Only well selected, not random reading, just to kill time, is feeding imagination, developing memory, and establishing new connections in the brain. Most importantly, it is developing a person's professional intelligence and competence.

3. <u>Try to learn any foreign language</u> for the first communication needs. Language learning is extremely beneficial against brain failures and dementia that hit very many middle aged and old people.

Language is the matrix of the brain; be sane!

4 <u>Learning classical poetry by heart</u> synchronizes our thinking with the authors. It identifies us with the self-worth of great world masters, develops our critical thinking skills, and boosts the sense of beauty that is very corrupted at present.

"Poetry is the highest type of Art!" (Belinsky)

Interestingly, the rhythm of poetry is harmonizing the brain. I'm not a poet, but I write the mind-sets that illustrate the concepts of all my books **in a rhyming form** because this is how they come to me. My students upload the ones they like most to their smart phones and use them if they need an inspirational boosting.

The poetic word charges the heart + mind cord!

5. Finally, **<u>you should do self-scanning in five dimensions.</u>** Do it in bed, before you fall asleep. Focus on how you started your day, who you saw, what you felt, said, did. <u>Be objective in your self-assessment</u>. Don't forget to thank God for your accomplishments or failures, if any. Practice the attitude of gratitude for any kind gesture of people around and practice kindness yourself.

Say "Hurray!" and Assess Yourself Every day!

8. Be God-Centered and Intelligence Absorbing! Be Self-Forming!

The neuroscience has it that the brain has a sophisticated apparatus of its own that <u>tracks our communal connections</u> and helps us navigate the world and establish connections with the people that we single out thanks to this ability. *"The brain creates the mental maps for us in terms of the physical space and complex social hierarchies and dynamics"* *("Brain"/ May-Britt Moser and Edward Moser, 2020)*

Make your brain unique, not bleak!

The present-day technological impact on our lives has brought us together to an unprecedented scope, and <u>it is the first time in our history that we realize our connection to the Universal Intelligence</u> not on a perceptual level that had always existed in us, but on the mental level, too. The existence of the Master Mind that we all call God remains questionable only for the uninformed ones. So, adjusting our **MENTAL ANTENNAS** to the vibrations of the Universe becomes an urgent need because it develops your individuality and. exceptionality.

"Freedom from the collective unconscious means freedom from emotional pain and futile suffering."(Carl Yung)

One must remember that people execute their own spells that destroy spirituality. Spirituality is not just acquiring a spiritual attitude of love for oneself and the life around us, <u>it is obtaining the life-constructing spirit that should be manifested through your brain.</u> Constantly developed intelligence of a person is filling him up with **a stronger spirit and a better reasoned out spirituality.** No wonder the mental dimension is the basis for the spiritual and universal levels in self-consciousness development. It explains why a person with undeveloped intelligence / wisdom cannot be connected to God, and his prayers are not heard. *(See the holistic paradigm above)*

"He Who Gets Wisdom Saves His Own Soul. "(Proverbs19 / 8)

9. Don't Think and Speak in Haste; It's Your Mind's Waste!

Being passionate about your dream does not mean being hasty. Self-Worth needs much **AWARE ATTENTION** development to life and living, not impulsive, inconsiderate thinking. Aware attention is based on the information that was properly *sifted for its validity and stored the brain* on the subject in question

Each decision needs stabilizing, harmonizing, and strategizing!

Slow thinking and speaking are not the indication of a person's mental inadequacy, but it's the mark of a deep self-worth commitment to finding the best solution of any problem based on accumulated intelligence and experience. To be properly solved any problem needs to be X-rayed in *the physical, emotional, mental, spiritual, and universal dimension.* A holistic approach develops intuition.

Enrich your intuition with mental fruition!

Haste destroys intuition , or *heart + mind link.* Together, they form the essential skill - aware attention that needs to be developed through life. Thus, *aware attention* paid to the five dimensions of the problem will help you see the light at the end of the tunnel. because it will enable you to see life holistically and accomplish success in your actions.

Systematize - Select - Analyze - Strategize - Actualize!

All self-worth and goal-oriented people focus their decisions on intuition that helps them stay unshaken in failure that occur on the path of light searching. Such people have the connection between the left, analytical brain, and the right, creative one. They have the **HOLISTIC MIND** that is one of a kind!

Intuition is the secret weapon of the right brain. Don't refrain!

Such People's Solution is treading the Path of Evolution!

10. My Global Role is to Holistically Reform My Soul!

Constantly strengthen your **self-worth steel** with the boosting induction

I Can! I Want to! And I will!

Before we move on toward further accumulation of self-worth in other dimensions, you need more **energy** and **motion**, or you need more

E-Motion!

To attain more **emotional energy** every time that your spirit sags for whatever reason, immediately fill up your mental-emotional tank with the **auto-inductive gas:**

I am a strong, bold, calm, and determined owner of my firm will!

I can (*You can finish this auto-induction according to your needs*)

I want to **manage my thoughts, words, feelings,**

And I will **and actions!**

I am becoming better and better with each coming day.

My Human Essence is in the Spiritual Renaissance!

In My Life Quest, I'm the Best!

Auto-Induction for a better Life Production:

To Be in Love with Self; Keep Surpassing Yourself!

11. Launch Yourself to the Life's Energy Spell! Don't Betray Yourself!

To launch yourself to action when a problem hits is a challenge that deplete us of the energy <u>and *weakens the spirit*</u> that is the most vital connecting part in **the spiritual fractal formation.** Remember, the goal of your life is <u>keeping the form and content of your being in sync</u>.

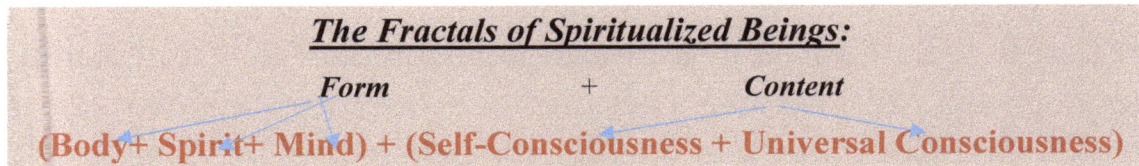

The Fractals of Spiritualized Beings:

Form   +   **Content**

(Body+ Spirit+ Mind) + (Self-Consciousness + Universal Consciousness)

We cannot affect the circumstances that are beyond our reach, but we can change the perception of them and our reaction to them. So, it's important <u>not to live inside the problem and allow yourself swim in it for a whole day</u>.

Don't dig into your feelings and dismiss the negative dealings. Start thinking about the vibrational cycle of your heartbeat *-21-21-21— Calm down; Calm -down; Calm down / So-o-o – Ha-a-am* . Accept the Rolla Costa rhythm of life and retain it with your spirit's might.

If you do not fake your feelings, you will improve your dealings!

Turn your disappointment, distress, insult, depression into life-obsession by turning on your confidence to discover the possibilities that this problem hides .**The problem loses its power over you, and you can resolve it, too!** The sense of self-worth will fortify your life's force and wouldn't let you become lethargic if you constantly scan it in five levels holistically.

The greatest spirit remains to be the spirit of the self-worthy Thee!

Remember, *your spiritual awakening* is an everyday job, and your thoughts are just the accumulation of the information that you have gathered so far. Sift the information for its validity, then process it.

Every Move is a Chore of Your Space-Time Life's Score!

12. Mobilize a Lot of Zest for Being the Best!

Concluding our talking about the mental enrichment of self-worth, I want to remind you that self-worth is getting formed thanks to *the mutation of all the levels in self-consciousness formation.*

There's no system without the structure!

So, self-worth formation is an on-going process of a personality development. You become a personality by means of *a titanic effort of will, self-discipline, and intelligence enrichment*. A business-like attitude to self-growth in all five dimensions must be established in your brain, and it must be checked daily without any compromises and justifications. Don't make empty plans without acting on them in a timely fashion. Don't betray yourself! Again,

"It's not enough to be the Best. Be the Only!" (Steve Jobs)

The present-day times provide us with endless sources of information, all kinds of seminars and You Tube talks by many advanced scientists, famous actors, and other self-made people who testify to the necessity of establishing self-control.

I suggest you apply whatever advice you get in all five levels every day, or at the *mini, meta, mezzo, macro, and super levels* of your business, love relationships, or any area of your life. Scanning yourself daily will become a new constructive habit.

You cannot run other people if you can't run yourself!

The method of *Selection + Organization = Self-Construction* (*Chunk 8 above*) will help your mind in processing every decision through the **GRID OF URGENCY**(*physical, emotional, mental, spiritual, universal),* sorting them out for their validity and urgency. Selection and organization of information become the basis for *self-worth gravity formation!*

Make Self-Worth Your Main Boss!

Stage Four

(The Spiritual Level of Self-Scanning)

Self-Worth

Refining!

A higher velocity of self-worth is our life's course!

Self-Induction:

In My Unbeatable Faith, I Exude a Lot of Grace!

Clear up Your Mind to Soul-Refine!

(Etienne Pirot)

You Belong to the Godly Spine!

1. Religiousness and Self-Worth are in Opposition Since Birth!

The spiritual level follows the mental level in my holistic paradigm of self-creation because one cannot **establish a conscious connection with the Universal Intelligences** without having a certain level of intelligence to be able to read and perceive the sacred texts without the help of a priest. So, **more than committing a sin**, we should fear becoming blindly ignorant. As Albert Einstein put it,

. **"Ignorance is still the worst enemy of the humanity!"**

The history of religion has impacted our lives for more than two thousand years, but we, as the top of the evolutionary development of life on Earth, have hardly become better. Many dogmatic maxima are still ruling our minds, separating us and making us wonder where the border line between religiousness and spirituality is. According to *Sadhguru's,* very wise definition, **"Religiousness is following the leader; spirituality is following the message!"** This is what is not being done now. Many people declare the belief in God, but they do not practice what their religion preaches, they do not seek God in them.

"Seek and you will find" if you do not betray your heart and the mind!

The existence of the Higher Power or the Master Mind that we all perceive as God is unquestionable now for the science and the most stubborn-thinking atheists. Albert Einstein's goal of life still mesmerizes us,. **"I want to know how God thinks - the rest is details."** As a matter of fact, **SELF-WORTH** development is the pivotal message in Christ's teachings. Specifically, he kept telling his disciples to look for the Heaven in themselves. **"I'm my own church!"** Sincere faith in God, not just sporadic praying, ritual visits to church, and the expectations to be heard in trouble **constitute God in our being, thinking, feeling, and seeing.** But faith is multi-dimensional, too.

To Be Connected to God, You Must Be Much More Mind-Developed!

2. Self-Worth is Connected to Christ's Media Force!

In my book, presenting the spiritual level of Self-Resurrection,*)* called *"Self-Taming"*(*www.language-fitness.com*), I ask the readers *to establish the referencing point* for their growing *spiritual intelligence* that should not be marred by blind, strictly normalized, and fake religiousness.

Self-worth is the internally spiritualized force!

Back in 1995, when I just came to the USA, I came across the *"Scientific American"* magazine with the image of Christ's face on the cover, taken by the computer imaging method *from the Turin Shrewd.* Since I had the seeds of faith instilled in me by my grandparents and my mom, I bought the magazine, made the copy of the image and placed it over my writing table.

The piercing eyes of Jesus Christ have become my referencing point since then, following me in my doubts and distress and giving me the spiritual boost that I could not get from anyone. My self-worth was tested by this sacred look, verifying my faith and the authenticity of my intentions, attitudes, and actions.

However, my belief was very weak and not rooted in any religious denomination. I have visited many churches that are at every corner, in the USA ,and I figured out that I did not feel comfortable in any of them because they reminded me of just businesses, based on the sacred faith in the Supreme Power, *but not necessarily practicing what they preach consciously.*

Being very scientifically oriented, I read a lot of sacred books and was able to interpret them without a priest's help. I have concluded that religion and science are just two sides of one coin that need *to be in my heart and mind together*, helping me stay authentic in my self-worth.

Inner Grace is My Main Self-Taming Device!

3. Negative Sensationalism is Killing Our Self-Growth Enthusiasm!

We live in a very negative social environment, full of meaningless, stupid commercials, negative fake news, tips on cooking that are filling up only the gut needs, not intellectual souls' seats.

There are too many violent, title-scary movies, cheap sex-based entertainment and children's cartoons that are filled up with arrogantly behaving ugly characters that with their angry sarcastic speaking are destroying the concepts of **BEAUTY AND HARMONY** in the minds and hearts of our kids and our own. According to Nikolas Roerich,

" Only consciously perceived beauty can save the humanity."

We are so lacking **AUTHENTICITY** and sincerity in life at large — in our communities, at our jobs, in our feelings and show-up behaviors that we stopped reacting consciously to the mess around us, perceiving life in "*a whatever way*" and repeating inwardly and outwardly:

"What do I care! I don't care! I care less!"

But we all must care because to evolutionary evolve with the technological make-up in stride, we need a wake-up call in the *physical, emotional, mental, spiritual, and universal realms of life* that is meant to bring openness and sincerity back into our hearts and minds. *The authenticity of the soul makes us whole!*

We all need a holistic **SELF-SCANNING** of every aspect of our common life in five levels because *every one's self-growth is also the society's qualitative change at every level*, irrespective of our class distinctions and race belongings. Keep repeating to yourself, *"Reject, resist, reform your inner de-form!"*

Self-Monitoring is the form of Self-Taming!

Constructive Evolutionary Change Must be Initiated on the Holistic Range!

4. We Need to Become More Spiritualized and Godly-wise!

Auto-Inductions:

My Body is My Temple,

My Mind is My Priest,

My Prayers are all Mental

My faith will never seize!

In My Everyday Life,

I manage to survive

With a Smile on My Face

And the Ever-Unbreakable faith!

By changing in the spiritual plane, we reform ourselves again and again! Let's start self-worth reformation with our language transformation because <u>*language is the portal of speech*</u> *that is often appalling both in form and the content.*

"Language is the skin of the soul!"

(Fernando L .Career)

"You are the Master of the Word that's Not said, but you're the Slave of the One that flew Ahead." *(Aram Hayami)*

5. Conscience Manifests in the Best!

Have you noticed that people of self-worth have *spiritualized intelligence* that shines from inside, irrespective of their skin color. By the way, when I came to this country, I met more people with a spiritual glee among the people of color than among the white Americans. The main rule of spirituality is observed by the best of them without any compromises and fakeness, with much grace, sincerity, and a ridged control over profanity.

They practice what they preach!

Science proves that true spirituality forms *an aura of protection* for the person of faith. That's why truly spiritual and intelligent people are not prejudiced. They are not black magic involved, or they are not relying on all kinds of predictions.

They know the true value of their faith, and *it protects their self-worth with the glee from inside*. Unfortunately, many people go to church every Sunday, sing and pray socially, but their souls are dirty, indifferent, and lacking conscience that is our second direct line to God They stop appreciating life in its authentic essence, and they are too preoccupied, displeased, discontent, and angry to see the beauty of it around. Faking faith is **FAKING LIFE!**

"At a certain point in life, most of us quit puzzling over everyday phenomena. We might savor the beauty of a blue sky, but we no longer bother to wonder why it is that color."(The Science of Creativity,2018).

You might not be perfect, but, irrespective of the fact whether you have been very consistent in self-worth accumulation or less so, *do not lose the perspective of self-bettering.* You are building *your own Cathedral* and allow me to help you lay some **BRICKS** of **CONSCIENCE** to make it more stable, solid, and indestructible. Conscience is the testing core of self-worth and much more!

Conscience is the Barometer of the Soul! It Makes Us Whole!

6. Bless People in Your Mind; Be One of a Kind!

To be One of a kind, or to become human gold, the One and the Only means to be bold and <u>to change your personal mold</u>, declaring to yourself and the world, ***I'm rising form my knees to fulfil my mind's and heart's needs!*** People of self-worth feel and think beyond the *"collective unconscious"* stereotyped perception of life that is based on money-chasing and fun-life glazing.

Don't rush to become biological trash!

Inner sacredness improves our spiritual link and put us with the Universe in sync! We get into the habit to verify our inner health with feeling blessed. We willingly give blessings to other people.

Long ago, I paid attention to the fact that the cross that we put on ourselves in blessing is, in fact, <u>the universal scientific sign</u> of our unifying with God or the Universal Intelligence in time and space. I wrote above that the central, vertical part of a cross is indicating ***the vector of time*** (*our past, present, future*), and the horizontal part of it is symbolizing ***the vector of space*** (*the process of life –* *the left minus end* and <u>*the result of life – the*</u> right positive end). (*See Stage Two,5*) <u>*Spiritually, the cross has the scientific value and a deep meaning.*</u>

The unity of the time and space is in every religious faith!

So, ***blessing ourselves and the loved ones with a cross***, <u>we are protecting ourselves and them in time and space</u>. Interestingly, the *Orthodox Christians* bless themselves, putting the cross from the right shoulder to the left one, while *the Catholics* position the cross from the left shoulder to the right one. I think that both blessings are God's protection, one - from the front (*the Orthodox blessing*) and the other one - from the back *(the Catholic blessing)*, *proving the unity of all religious divisions in their sacred holistic sense.* We bless our kids from left to right to make them better protected with the God's cross.

The Art of Blessing is the Art of Connecting!

7. Demagnetization of Self-Worth

It is an accepted fact that it is easy to say, *"Stay away from the poison of life!"* But doing it requires character! To be successful in this very challenging goal, we must first learn to resist the temptation and then **to magnetize our inner core with new values.**

Live by the moral code; Love is our spiritual mold!

I have noted above and I want to accentuate it again that we e need *"to reverse the triple 666*, signifying **sex+ body+ mind** to *the triple 999"*, or **mind+ body + sex.** In the celestial terms, we need to change the evil, a badly willed side of us into the divine one that is still there but got weak due to the lack of willpower and faith. *"Most of us spend our lives bouncing back and forth between the good and the bad sides of life."(Ravi. P. S. Berg).* **"Be activated by the internal influences for the external responses.***"(Edgar Cayce)* .Don't belong to the *"collective unconscious.*" *(Carl Yung)* Play a solo role in that concert.

.Be unique, personable, and charismatic! Be a New You!

Launch yourself back to your exceptionality every day by heightening the voltage of your spirit auto--suggestively*! "Re-program your cells."* **Be yourself!** *(Dr. Bruce Lipton) (See Stage One,4)*

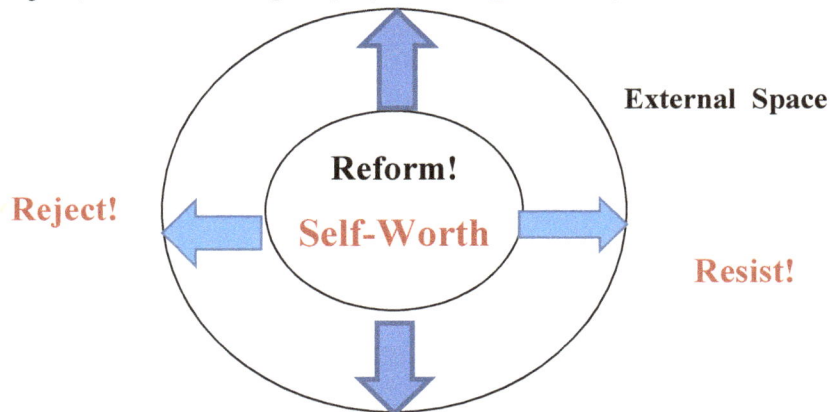

Reject! — Reform! Self-Worth — Resist! — External Space

Reject, Resist, and Reform to Obtain a New Life's Uniform!

8. Habits Stability Needs to be Turned into Skills' Nobility!

In my book " *Self-Taming,* " featuring the spiritual self-growth, I have outlined the steps of <u>self-assessing and self-correcting</u>, based on the **SELF-TAMING SKILLS** that we need to develop in ourselves throughout life. The title page of the book contains the picture of Jesus Christ that has become mt referencing point for self-worth.

I have been in the USA for a year then and my life was in shambles - divorce with the husband of 25 years of the wedlock, no experience of living in a brutal capitalist world, no knowledge of how to adjust to it and how nose my self-worth in the turmoil of new life It's then that I have made up the first prayer for myself.

> *God is at my right side; Christ is at my left side.*
>
> *Light is inside! Light is My Might!*

The piercing eyes of Jesus Christ became my referencing point of grace and sincerity, backing me up in any trouble and tribulation in life. Thanks to it, I obtained new <u>inner strength, self-reliance, and self-sufficiency</u>.

I stopped seeking anyone's support and seized complaining and victimizing myself. I *have "planted" Christ's nobility and His piercing look,* following me everywhere into my soul. I have learned to process my life through the *physical, emotional, mental, spiritual, and universal realms in sync,* <u>giving the objective assessment</u> of my accomplishments at each level. Life started taking the right vector. <u>***I've stopped being just a survivor. I've become my life-modifier!***</u>

Form + *Content*

(Body+ Spirit+ Mind) + (Self-Consciousness + Universal Consciousness)

"Seek and You Will Find" if You Unite the Heart, the Spirit and the Mind!

9. Your Personal Goal's Right is the Spiritual Might!

Our common goal in life is *to log on our biological computers* to the *Universal Information Field (Dr .John Hagelin),* or to the Master Computer and to follow our calling. You realize what your goal in life is if you manage *to discover your exceptionality,* the realization of which becomes your true **MISSION ON EARTH** .

Spiritual growth is the way of installing your self-worth on Earth!

This universally governed process depends on the level of your conscious spiritual and intellectual development, or *on the level of your self-consciousness and the sense of your self-worth.*

Regrettably, *"the majority of the people on Earth sees the world through grey contact lenses, and only the people with a high level of consciousness can enjoy life in the kaleidoscope of its colors."* *(Tikhoplav V. U. and T. S)*

That's very right because we are the same in our weaknesses, *but unique in your strengths.* Your exceptionality gets revealed in your interests, aspirations, and special skills that magnetize our self-worth with the ability to make a difference in the world, following the goal that takes shape in the process of realization *who and what you are!* That's why we tend to gravitate to the best, following their self-worth committed fest!

With God in the heart and the mind,

We get united as One,

In yin and yang,

In Earth, Water, Air, and the Sun.

Each of us becomes a Universal One!

Everyone is Precious and Unique, And This is How You Need to Think!

10. Outshine Those That are Vile! Shine!

To resist the evil forces around you, try *to be authentic and whole physically, emotionally, mentally, spiritually, and universally*. Don't play anyone's role! Be true to your self-value and never betray it under any circumstances. People play games, lie a lot about themselves to look better in someone's eyes, and dim their inner light with negative thoughts, feelings, and actions.

Authenticity is the best weapon against negativity!

We cannot but admit that the general public is affected by pretentiousness and showing off, as if everyone is living in the make-believe fun world, full of sleazy jokes, profanity, and .sarcasm. Picking at each other, ironizing and amusing oneself with being listened to has become a norm.

But your self-worth is more spiritual than attitudinal!

I have the impression that stupid advertising and commercials are truly programming people's fake behaviors. Why don't we come back into our authentic forms and try to perfect them to the point that will make people gravitate to us, without our trying to stand out thanks to the tattoos, pierced ears or lips. Our churches are full of people that light candles and pray with a humble look on their faces, but their real actions often show the other side of such fake religiousness.

A person shines only when he is true to himself in his inner cell!

No doubt, to be closer to God, *you need to reduce the fake pretentiousness and negative self-talk!* Release your worries into God's hands! Solutions are His magic wands!

When we are true to ourselves, we are true to our faith and sincere in our prayers to God. Only then **does *intuition become our sacred sanitizer*** that makes us cleaner and wiser!

Your Self-Worth needs an Authentic Self-Growth!

11. Praying is Self-Worth Gaining!

When we are praying,

We're self- worth gaining!

Remembering God,

We're building up the Spiritual Fort!

We're becoming lighter

And mind-brighter!

We enforce the Christ's force

And put evil in reverse!

Christ in unity with you

Makes the shield of the Two!

We feel protected by God

With His everlasting support!

We're standing up from our knees

And charge our cells with Christ's deeds!

We're uplifting ourselves to the spiritual heights

And conquer millions of web sites!

With Christ's word in Thee

You're full of the godly glee!

Let God Be Magnetized to Me!

Let Me Be! Let Me Be! Let Me Be!

12. Idealism is Our Best Self-Forming "izm"!

To conclude reviewing the value of self-worth on the spiritual plane, let me confess that I like people who idealize life and believe in the best in people. I'm not talking about perfectionists here, but of regular people, able **to simplify their life and not to tread anyone's track**. Such people are not led by their hormones, limiting their intelligence and compromising self-worth.

The unanimity of Self is the core of a personal cell!

To retain **SELF-SANITY**, we need to sustain the unanimity of the *physical, emotional, ,mental, spiritual, and universal realms* in ourselves, constantly scanning our souls for their holistic unity with the reality of life at large. I have a deep respect for a very good Canadian actor, *Keanu Reeves* who has a very distinct self-worth and retains his own picture of the present-day reality without a fake self-presentation.

"I hate the world where husbands dress their wives as prostitutes, displaying what needs to be sacred. I hate the world which has no sense of honesty and dignity, where women don't want to have children and men don't want to have a family, where teenagers show off at the wheel of their dad's cars and anyone who has a little power tries to put you down, where people declare hypocritically that they believe in God, not knowing the first thing about their religion."

This true picture of self-worth is resonating in my mind and heart because many people live as if they are rehearsing their lives, and real life will be lived by them sometime in the future. Accumulating the negligent days, months, years, loves, casually done jobs, and poorly raised children, they are piling up the karmic energy that, in the end, is going to tears them down and leave much emptiness inside about the aimlessly lived lives. *Meanwhile, we are shaping the future Now!*

Don't Be Evil-Bewitched; Practice What Your Preach!

Stage Five

(The Universal Level of Self-Scanning)

Self-Worth
Salvation!

Salvation is looking up to the Sun of Creation!

Be a Great Human Being - A Miracle of Living!

To Self-Excel, Build up a Universal Domain in Yourself!

The Salvation of My Soul is the Cradle for My Goal!

(A French Sculptor -Etienne Pirot)

In the Cradle of My Life, It Must Eternally Survive!

1. The Soul's Salvation is in Your Universal Realization!

"A Genius is a Man who realized his Mission in life." *(Goethe)*

Remember, we are not alone in the Universe, never have been! So, learn to tune yourself up to the station "God," or the Universal Intelligence that's our common Fort!

With God, uniting us as One,

We are centered in the Sun!

In yin and yang,

Earth, Water, Air, and the Sun,

I'm becoming a Universal One!

I accept my life in its entire mass

For it, too, Shall Pass!

The universal people are like birds.

They are flying in their minds' outskirts!

Being the Best is a Life-Long Quest!

2. Universal Awakening is the Path of the Elite Minds

Our universal awakening is directly connected to self-worth formation and self-consciousness development. ___This is the top, universal level of personality development___ with the highest personal magnetism attained, and only the best of the best, the most life-purpose dedicated people can be qualified as the **Self-Resurrected** ones.

Who and what you identify yourself with determines your life's bliss!

The contribution of these people's self-worth to the planet Earth is beyond any doubt because it has changed the way people think and live. The self-worth of **Nikola Tesla, Steve Jobs, Elon Musk, Oprah Winfrey** and many other exceptional people like them does not come across as just cool or super-charismatic to whet the appetites of the crowd, corrupted by the life -sensationalizing mass media.

Their in-put into the world evolution is their life's solution!

It's already beyond the terrestrial! It's recorded in the universe because it was exceptionally giving and mind-reforming, it is ever aspirational and psychologically gravitational .*Self-worth gravity of the people of the universal level of self-realization is a true sensation!*

They don't have a negligent attitude to life because they have the sense of time and space in sync. They are aware of the fact that the betrayal of one's goal in life generates karma accumulation that is often the result of compulsive, unconscious actions. Self-growth unmotivated people, on the contrary, don't want to be patient with life; they want the result of the "*immediate gratification*" whim in their life stream. Unfortunately, there are very many down-to-earth, not **"up-to-earth"** people. The universal goal of full **realization of one's exceptionality as the life's mission** is often secondary for them, if considered at all.

Don't Be Life-Negligent; Be Life-Intelligent!

3. Integrity is the Wholeness of Oneness!

So, building up self-worth in the universal dimension is the final , a very challenging and the most honorable step on the ladder of self-growth. The personal impact of the people who complete their Self-Resurrection or Self-Salvation is really sensational.

It's human spirit elevating and holistically captivating!

Their ascending the stairway of Self-Resurrection is always full of falls and failures, but their *personal magnetism* is so strong that no obstacles, created by the ignorance of people and the evil at work can stop them from accomplishing their mission.

The universality of" the best and the only" keeps us captivated and more goal-oriented!

The holistic paradigm of the exceptional people is the same , but "to *go beyond, fully beyond, completely beyond"* can manage only the *physically, emotionally, mentally, and spiritually bold ones* ones that follow this path holistically and consciously.

The *physical dimension* is based on the emotional make-up. *The emotional core* is formed by the intelligence of a person, which is *the mental level* of self-growth. Intelligence is inevitably evolving into *self-enlightenment* (*the spiritual level).*

Finally, a person's spirituality is growing into the **UNIVERSALITY** of **SELF-IDENTIFICATION**. *(the universal level).* So, every one of us has the same choice to make - *to exist as a part of the Universal Creation or to survive as life's waste* with may regrets. Apparently, to be successful, anyone's life must be based on a clear-cut plan of action and the clarity of thinking in its realization.

"Go Beyond, Fully Beyond, Completely Beyond!" (The Buddhist Mantra)

4. Be Bold! Reshape the Society - Programmed Mold!

Self-worth is a very personal force that is manageable only for strong spirits. Meanwhile, <u>being authentic, sincere, and honest</u> has become a weird concept, rejected by most people as freaky. *Being true to oneself is a very difficult proposition* because we have all been molded since childhood by the family, school, college, job and relationships that have left many scars on our psyche. Cutting s loose from their joint impact for the sake of self-growth appears to be unsurmountable for many characterless people, to say the least. Obviously, striking the balance between public and personal is helping to ascertain who you are.

"Be the thing in itself."(Hegel) Be Yourself!

When the necessity to reform the inner deform hits us, or *the period of enlightenments arrives,* we feel depleted by the inner negative forces of resistance. I call this period of awakening the time of **SELF-TAMING** and life-gaining with self-benefiting growth of life inside..

I like the book "***Right is Might***" by *Richard Wetherill* that teaches us not to be led by what we like and what we expect to happen, but to follow the <u>life-formed skills of the right behavior of the winner spirit fortification.</u> Only then, the sense of universal freedom is growing inside, forming an unbreakable *heart + mind unity.*

Freedom outside starts with killing the spirit of a slave inside!

A great Russian writer, *Anton Chekhov* called on people "***to start squeezing the spirit of a slave***" in themselves "***drop by drop.***" This is what a truly self-worthy person does. A self-worthy person is always free-spirited, insightful, constantly learning and perfecting himself in the *physical, emotional, ,mental, spiritual, and universal dimensions* of life and living. Most certainly, they are **ORDER-ORIENTED,** too because it's impossible to maintain order in the head without having it around. *The orderly life outside eliminates chaos inside!*

Life Gaining is in Self-Taming!

5. To Get the Universal Inkling, Change the Culture of Your Thinking!

The world is changing toward its *universal awakening in time and space,* and new times demands *a new , inclusive vision of the reality* and the necessity to work out a new mechanism of responding to it.To become a sculptor and a choreographer of your life, you need to master the reflective thinking art. Slow, reflective , holistically strategized thinking <u>helps synchronize the left and right hemispheres of the brain,</u> promoting our evolutionary growth. *Mind + Heart Link must be with the Universal Intelligence in sync,* and the use of technology is helping to tune in to it for those who have" *eyes to see and ears to hear".*

Sporadic thinking and automatic treatment of life is turning mindless people into savages, driven by low instincts, emotionally uncontrolled reactions, money-chasing, and irresponsible treatment of each other. To re-educate our young people in *the art of disciplined thinking and controlled language processing* is our priority on the path of our evolving beyond the terrestrial boundaries of the impossible!

 Also, growing holistically in the previous four dimensions, we'll manage to command the **ART** of **SELF-ANALYSIS,** mastering of which will <u>eradicate self-justifying and the lack of self-refining.</u> How, for example, can our children *to be self-taming and self-tamed* if they are enjoying the shows that promote shamelessness, profanity, tongue-lashing, and ruthless, disgusting manners, cheered by the crowd. Hence, their souls are barren for the seeds of inner grace and true faith.

Education is not just learning, it's also self-forming!

There are *two basic qualities* that form our resistance to evil and bad, explosive reactions to life. *They are self-awareness and a true sense of self-worth!* It's beneath your self-worth to be so down-to-earth!

Sculpture Yourself up! Be a Pygmalion of Your Life!

6. Don't Let Anyone Erode Your Spirit's Mold!

Everyone has his / her own self-worth processed *from egoism to altruism*. The most significant thing in this process is the right of every person around you at home, at work, in the street, or in the church to declare his individuality and exceptionalism. Again, use the induction:

I'm my Best Friend; I'm my Beginning and my End!

Growing on *the path of universality*, try to perceive the people around you as your equals, your contemporaries that have come to the world as temporary visitors, too. Help, empower, enlighten, and grow the self-worth together. Self-overpowering is the process of taming our stereotyped, subjective thinking, judgmental attitudes, and uncontrolled behaviors. Taming them, *you'll instill new objective values into the subjective mind* and refine your marred soul.

Let inclusive love, care, and compassion come back in fashion!

To become more self and life-content, have a kind, sincere, open-hearted attitude to people, and they will pay you back with their gratitude and the smile that *uplifts the spirit to the spiritual heights of the infinity of life.* Be sure to induct your mind and heart with the mind-set of mutual respect, granted to the people around you.:

Respect is Me; Respect is my Philosophy!

On the holistic path of self-resurrection, your dream must be an irreversible wish to realize your unique potential without expecting someone *to discover your exceptionality* that is the seed of your dream, elevating your spirit and helping you justify the gift of life granted to you. Get out of your society-programmed cell! *You are a universal being with a new vision of Self-Seeing!* To boost yourself, keep programming every cell,

I Can Roam Any Terrain with the Godly Attitude in My Vein!

7. Launch the Program of Elation and Rejuvenation!

As is mentioned above, self-growth is the process of five-dimensional transforming us into **NEW BEINGS**, able to live freely and happily in any circumstances. *Self-Awareness* that we need to obtain as early as possible rejuvenates the wish to realize the God-given potential, granted to us from the Above.

We are meant to process new self-knowledge through the stages of emotional **S***elf-Monitoring*, professional *Self-Installation*, spiritual, **S***elf-Realization*, and universal *Self-Salvation*. So, transform yourself in the *"space you are in. and the time that is given to you."* (Albert Einstein)

Spiritual formation means your spirit's transformation!

Active self-programming or *the Auto-Suggestive Meditation* that all my books are based help accumulating your **SELF-WORTH** in the *physical, emotional, mental, spiritual, and universal levels* holistically, inducted at the cellular of the fractal self-creation.

(Body+ Spirit+ Mind) + (Self-Consciousness + Universal Consciousness)

It's vital to boost the spirit that connects the mind and the body and helps you raise your self-consciousness inwardly at the cellular level in a new, much more aware way. A digital biologist *Dr. Bruce Lipton* whom I have quoted above on this subject says,

"We need to change the biology of our beliefs on the cellular level"

Life demands that we change our focus from the old knowledge to the new one and acquire *the holistic level of life-awareness,* rationalizing our lives and charging the personal informational field around us consciously to become better connected to *the Universal Informational Field* that is managing our lives digitally now.

Long Live the Beat of "So Be It!"

8. Scientific Literacy is Needed Now - WOW!

Dr. Bruce Lipton proves also that much of our old knowledge is outdated and needs to be refined. Therefore, our professional. *Self-Installation* (*mental level of self-growth*) must be considerably enriched with new, technologically enhanced knowledge about every branch of science that is transforming the most advanced minds considerably now.

The third stage of professional self-installation is outlined in the book *"Living Intelligence and the Art of Becoming,"* and it presents the ten essential vistas of intelligence that we need to mount in the same five levels *physical, emotional, mental, spiritual, and universal* to consider ourselves able to go with the flow of an exponentially growing technology that provide new breakthroughs in science. (*See the global award-winning book on intelligence-www. language-fitness.com*)

Uniting all the levels of our self-growth in the evolutionally process of *Self-Salvation,* we will be better going in accord with the future developments of life on earth. We need much more *"scientific literacy"* and the objective knowledge of the life on Earth and beyond it. So, help your mind be One with the Universal Mind of the Sun! Be a part of new thinking, seeing, acting and feeling!

Prefer eternal flying to common dying! Be a Universal Being!

"Scientific literacy demands that we know the laws of nature. We need to inspire ourselves to know how the world works."

(*Neil deGrasse Tyson*)

" Scientific knowledge is the origin of our future consciousness!"

(*Elon Musk*)

Let Your Mind Travel Freely!

9.Self-Scanning is Self-Worth Refining!

(An Inspirational Booster)

Every day, when you are without any mask,

You must address yourself and ask,

"What have I done today

For my physical array?

Have I added a bit

To my emotional upbeat?

Have I enriched

My mental out-reach?

And , finally, on the spiritual plane,

Have I gotten closer to God's domain?"

So, don't waste your daily zest

To just possess!

Use it to infuse

Your self-realization fuse!

Ration your Self-Taming Concentration!

Your Life's Goal is the Aristocratism of the Soul!

10. The Matrix of Self-Worth Formation

Living Intelligence + *Enlightened Self-Consciousness*

Form **+** **Content**

(Body+ Spirit+ Mind) + (Self-Consciousness + Universal Consciousness)

Physical , emotional, mental, spiritual, and universal realms of life

= A whole, spiritually intellectualized Self!

The Ladder of Self-Resurrection:

Super level	**Super Consciousness**	***Self-Salvation***
Macro level	**Self-Consciousness**	***Self-Realization***
Mezzo level	**Mind**	***Self- Installation***
Meta level	**Spirit**	***Self-Monitoring***
Mini level	**Body**	***Self- Knowledge***

The link of the physical + emotional + mental + spiritual + universal force determines your Life's Course!

"When a person knows his mission on earth, he lives most purposefully and effectively." (Leo Vygotsky)

There is no System without the Structure!

Make your decisions in life, using both hemispheres of the brain - analytical and systemic. Process your mind through the systemic paradigm *(physical, emotional, mental, spiritual, and universal)* to get the holistic picture of life that you must be constructing with your solid sense of Self-Worth on the Planet Earth!

To Life-Stride, Raise Your Self-Consciousness in Life!

11. Accept Your Life in its Entire Mass for "It too Shall Pass!"

Concluding the book, let me remind you again that only with the *rationalization of the value of life* and a *conscious use of technology* that feeds our thinking now can we deal with the tribulations of life both de facto and de juror. They are an inseparable part of the entropy process that goes together with the evolution on the universal plane.

The process of knowing is endless, and it is a great honor to say, like Socrates," *I know I know nothing, the rest don't know even that!"* So, let's consciously tune to new knowledge vibrations, intelligence reformations, and scientific innovations.

In our quest for the meaning of *the conceptual structure of life,* we are learning to decipher the digital text that is transmitted to us from the Above. Naturally, more emotionally refined and intelligence-advanced people will not sacrifice their self-worth for an immediate, mind-blurring pleasure.

The present-day market is suffocating without such people and our education must provide them. Conscious holistic *self-reflection* and s*elf-assessment* are the irreplaceable tools in such evolution of a human soul that raises its self-worth on the planet Earth.

Obviously, our kids should study the" *Art of Being and Becoming"* or the **SCIENCE OF LIFE** as one of the most essential subjects in school and as a supplementary one in their academic future. Look at the crowds of people that life-coaching professionals gather. The hunger for unanswered life questions is insatiable, the interest in science is growing by the day, and the sources are all there, at our fingertips.

Being Better Informed, You Become Universally Portent!

Conclusion of the Self-Worth Infusion

Internalize Your Emotions,

But Externalize the Mind!

Be One of a Kind!

Self-Induction:

Self-Worth is My Inner Boss!

I Declare to Thee:
" I'm the Whole Me; I'm the Best I Could Ever Be!"

(A great French sculptor - Etienne Pirot)

Share Your Self-Worth! Make the World Better, Not Worse!

1. To Live or to Survive? - That's the Question of the Present-day Life!

Concluding the book, thank you wholeheartedly for having read it that far and having reasoned out the major concepts of it - *your Self-Worth is the unification of your soul and consciousness,* the methodology of which I've touched upon in five dimensions above.

Sharpen and focus your aware attention to get to the Higher Consciousness dimension!

I want to reiterate the idea that there is no personal evolution possible without your constructive work on self-love, intellectual self-installation, constant self-adjustment, and possibly, total self-realization. Indeed, to attain a permanent mastery over your life, you must change the nature of your thoughts and behaviors, that is,

YOU MUST ADOPT A NEW CULTURE OF THINKING!

Each stage of a personality development is connected to the next or the previous one. The process of **SELF-EVOLUTION** is gradual and most rewarding because you become free of the *"collective unconscious,"* or the crowd mentality, and you no longer depend on your weaknesses and misgivings, your past mistakes and the criticism of the immediate human environment.

There is another aspect to it. *You are an integral part of all that is!* You are not an isolated entity in the Universe anymore.

You are on the God's shore!

We all need to uplift ourselves beyond the boundaries of common-sense life by assimilating the accumulated knowledge holistically and probing the puzzling enigma of life in the universe, creating our own *intellectually spiritualized fractals of being.*

Don't Have Any Fear! You Can Conquer the Pamir!

2. Your Self-Viability Must Be in Holistic Unity!

My five books on **Self-Resurrection** and the two featuring love in five dimensions and the importance of accumulating the sense of self-worth are my modest attempt to create an inspirational, systematized **MANUAL OF LIFE** in the *physical, emotional, mental, spiritual, and universal realms of our technologically enhanced life now.* .A simple blueprint at hand will <u>help you overcome the inertia of the mindless life sight velocity around you.</u>

"Those that have eyes see; those that have ears hear."

Spiritual listening that we develop through meditation and self-inducting opens the lines of communication with the Universal Intelligence, and it paves the way to your **SELF-VIABILITY.** It releases the soul from being barred in the robotically operating and spiritually disconnected mind–body form. If you focus on your intuition and take time to tune up your **AUTO-ANTENNA** *to the station "God" that is Inside, Above and Beyond,* you will gradually establish the connection with the life inside, protecting your self-worth as an intellectually spiritualized force.

Focusing on the life within becomes our Meditative Gene!

You need to stay on the same wavelength, establish *a* **MIND-TO-MIND** and **HEART-TO-HEART** contact with the Universe and with the people that cross your life path in a meaningful way. <u>Your conscience will protect you from the pains of remorse and the ruins of self-worth!</u> To be present in the moment is to be *"the watcher of your mind, your thoughts, your speech, and your emotions."*(Deepak Chopra) Your thinking, feeling and acting will follow the systemic paradigm, *Synthesis - Analysis - Synthesis! (books on Self-Resurrection)*

Good Input Results into a Good Output!

2. Generalize - Select - Internalize - Strategize - Actualize! Be Wise!

Sorting out the new life's in-put consciously with *aware attention* to yourself and the people around, you will stop speaking or listening *in the somnambulistic state of a mind* that works on the automatic pilot, unconsciously. By upgrading the trust in your intuition, you'll get rid of the habit of immediate gratification, fake emotions, and corruptive beliefs that need conscious taming and transforming.

Protect your Self-Worth Fort; stay aboard!

To accomplish that, sort out the redundant information bombarding you from the outside world - the electronic gadgets, TV, or robotized people. The work at the **SOUL'S ECOLOGY** is a lifelong commitment! It never ends because our souls need food for thought and love for the heart to sustain its qualities eternally.

Heart + Mind Unity = the Soul's Purity!

Therefore, in all books on Self-Resurrection, you will find more *inspirational boosters* that can help you recycle the bothering you habits consciously, choosing the ones that are more workable and systemically life-bound *physically, emotionally, mentally, spiritually, and universally.* Recycling holistically your **SELF-WORTH** is the essential part of the spiritual recovery and maturation. You need to study the book and work through the cook, following its holistic paradigm in any problematic life situation that needs the right solution.

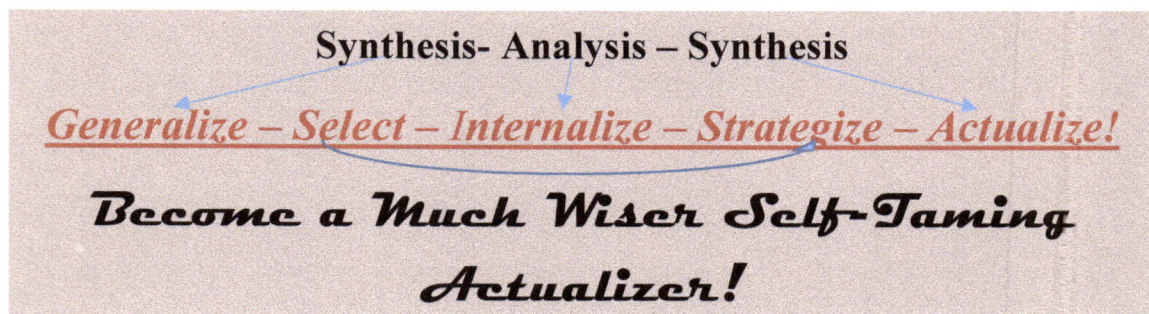

Synthesis- Analysis – Synthesis

Generalize – Select – Internalize – Strategize – Actualize!

Become a Much Wiser Self-Taming Actualizer!

4. Everyone Has a Magic Wand – God's Words at Hand!

So, the book" *Self-Worth*" is meant to help you become more life-aware and _more luminous_ in life. You ae the individual with your exceptional identity and the inner light that you are willing to share with your loved ones and the people around you.

Your inner light is meant to solidify your Self-Worth

on the planet Earth!

All of us must process ancient wisdom and the selected God's words through a new technologically enhanced vision of life in its eternal values.

Life is a limited gift for every one of us, and it should be used to perfect oneself so that, leaving this world, we could feel no regrets for having wasted this gift .

Don't take life for granted; it's God granted!

I, for one, read one of the thirty-one *Proverbs* in the Bible every day, thinking that each of them is connected to the corresponding date of the month.

Surprisingly, even though the same dates are repeated each month, I find new wisdoms that help me resolve my problems on that day. **King Solomon's wisdoms** have become my everyday directions and the helping hand for the solutions of any problem.

Hopefully, the book "*Self-Worth* "will help you revive the wish to justify your life and feel accomplished in it, irrespective of all the troubles and tribulations that life casts on your path. The rule of your life must remain the same:

"Life is Tough, but I'm Tougher!"

5. Your Luminosity is in the Self-Worth Velocity!

Having rewired your **HEART + MIND** connection, and having substantially raised your self-consciousness, <u>you'll start perceiving God differently</u> because you'll be way closer to the Universal Intelligence that we call God in every thought, word, and action.

So, get connected to the station" God" for His everlasting support!

The digital **ANTENNA** of our connection to the Universal Intelligence helps transmit the instructions of wisdom in the form of the direct line to God - *your intuition*.

The goal of self-creation at the new time and space location is urgent for all of us, and postponement of adding a few positive traits to our lives cannot be excusable because the exponential growth of technology will just sweep the lazy ones off *"the surface of life beyond survive"*.

<u>*So, let's go with the flow of the technological grow!*</u>

"Life is Just a Moment

Of Our Dissolution

In Everyone and Everything

As a Gift of Self-Solution!"

Your Soul is a Universal Perpetua Mobile!

Life is Just a Time-Space Speck;
Don't Waste its Unstoppable" Beg!"

(Speedy running in Russian)

(A Runner- A Greek Sculptor - Kostos Varotsos /Athens)

Speed is Me; Speed is My Infinity!

6. Don't Ever Turn off the Light in Your Soul! Stay Whole!

Finally, if you live in the Sun, no one can do you any harm!

So, Be in Unity with your Inner Divinity!

Inner divinity means conscious living and learning. It's everyday self-scanning through the grid of urgency and retaining your personal magnetism in any life circumstances.

Personal charisma is not a God-given exceptional quality.

It crowns the most successful people, good money-makers, and excellent givers and life-reformers. It's the result of a goal-oriented, self-disciplined, and constantly self-magnetized spirit that the people charge on a regular basis not to let anyone or anything de-magnetize their self-worth and makes it worthless. in any of the five levels of life: *physical, emotional, mental, spiritual, and universal!*

It's truly amazing how **INNER GRACE,** the very core of self-worth, becomes handy in difficult situations. Grace is your guardian angel that wouldn't let you humiliate yourself with yelling, tongue-lashing, uncontrolled anger, cheating, greed , or violence.

Any person of self- worth will never downgrade himself / herself with *turning off the light* of his or any one's soul in any nerving or tempting situation.

I love this country for its international make-up that allows me to see *the spark of true inner grace* in the people from all over the world, irrespective of their skin color, national background, religious affiliation, or political views.

As *Don Miguel* Ruiz writes in his wonderful book *"The Four Agreements,"*

"Under Any Circumstances, always Do Your Best - No More and No Less!"

7. The Route of Self-Resurrection Must Be Completed Section by Section!

In sum, having done a substantial self-scanning, raised your self-awareness, enriched your self-knowledge, and fortified your self-love, be sure to boost your spirit with the accomplishments at five levels of your *self-worth formation and self-creation:*

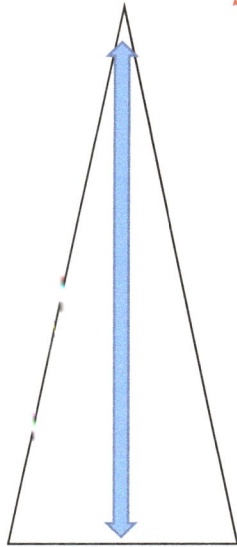

Stages of Spiritual Maturation and Self Refinement:

Universal Connection	**Self-Salvation**	*Universal Dimension*
Spiritual Maturity	**Self-Realization**	*Spiritual Dimension*
Mental Awareness	**Self-Installation**	*Mental Dimension*
Emotional Control	**Self- Monitoring**	*Emotional Dimension*
Physical Fitness	**Self-Knowledge**	*Physical Dimension*

Your Destination is a Happy Life's Elation!

I admit - I am physically fit!

I admit - I am emotionally fit!

I admit - I am mentally fit!

I admit - I am spiritually fit!

I admit - I am universally fit!

I Have Accomplished the Goal of Making Myself Whole!

8. My Final Self-Induction

So, Plug into the Void

Inside You,

Feel the Sacredness

of IS;

Learn the Power of

NOW

And enjoy Life

AS IS!

Keep on Becoming and Soul-Refining!

Turn on the Sun of Your Soul;

Be Happy and Whole!

9. The Panegyric to God!

(An Inspirational Booster)

I'm singing the panegyric to God

For His everlasting support;

For the chance to live

And the happiness to think and to perceive;

For the miracle to smile

And wash my face in the sun rays for a while;

For the happiness to love

And to pass the gift of life from the Above;

For the light and darkness,

For my stupidity and smartness;

For the right and wrong,

For the evil and good that I perform;

For the music of my heart,

For the Sun, the Moon, and my strong gut!

I thank God for all at once,

Every morning, not just once!

Don't Take Life for Granted,
It is God Granted!

Dr. Ray with Her Inspirational Say!

1. *"Emotional Diplomacy or Follow the Bliss of the Uncatchable Is!"/ Editorial LEIRIS, New York, USA,2010*

2. *"Four Dimensions of a Soul"* *(Auto-Suggestive Psychology in Russian) / LEIRIS Publishing, New York, USA,2011*

3. *"Americanize Your Language, Emotionalize Your Speech!"* */ Nova Press, USA, 2011*

4. *"It Too Shall Pass!"* *(Inspirational Boosters in Four Dimensions) / Xlibris, 2012*

5. *"I am Strong in My Spirit!"* *(Inspirational Boosters in Russian) / Xlibris, 2013.*

6. *"Language Intelligence or Universal English"* *(Method of the Right Language Behavior),* *Book One* */Xlibris, 2013 - Also, Stonewallpress,2019*

7. *"Language Intelligence or Universal English"* *(Remedy Your Language Habits,"* *Book Two* */Xlibris, 2013 – Also, Stonewallpress,2019*

8. *"Language Intelligence or Universal English,"* *(Remedy Your Speech Skills)* *Book Three* */Xlibris, 2013- Also, Stonewallpress,2019*

9. *"My Solar System,"* *(Auto-Suggestive Psychology for Inner Ecology) Xlibris, 2015*

The Books on Self-Resurrection:

10. *"I Am Free to Be the Best of Me!"- (Physical Dimension) -* *Toplinkpublishing.com. Sept. 2017) – Second Edition , Book Whip, 2019*

11. *Soul-Refining! (Emotional Dimension) (Toplinkpublishing.com. May 2017) - Second Edition , Book Whip, 2019*

12. *"Living Intelligence or the Art of Becoming"(Mental Dimension)- (A New Paradigm of Self-Creation) Xlibris, 2015 - Second Edition , Bookwhip,2019*

13. *"Self-Taming" (Life-Gaining is in Self-Taming!)(Spiritual Dimension)- Book Whip, 2019*

14. *" Beyond the Terrestrial!"* *(Be the Station for Self-Inspiration!) - (Universal Dimension) Xlibris, June 2016- Second Edition -, Book Whip, 2019*

15. *"Beyond the Terrestrial!" – Third Edition - URLink Print and Media, 2019*

16. *" The State of Love from the Above!"- Book Whip, 2019 / "Love Ecology"- Second edition- Prime Solutions.*

www. Language – fitness.com

email; - dr.rimaletta@gmail.com / dr.rimalettaray369 @outlook.com / **Tel. (203) 212-2673**